Praise for *The Pricing Sprint*

'Most pricing books either get lost in theory or reduce pricing to tactics. *The Pricing Sprint* avoids both traps. It offers a clear, structured, and refreshingly human way of tackling pricing — grounded in real decisions teams face, not abstract models.'

Maciej Kraus, Partner at Movens Capital and Pricing Lecturer at Stanford University

'Finally, a clear and practical guide to the most overlooked lever in business success: pricing. This book shows exactly how to get it right.'

Murray Lambell, CCO, Gousto

'This book short-circuits years of costly guesswork and materially accelerates growth.'

Alexander von Schirmeister, former Managing Director, Xero

'A confident business knows how to talk about price. This book helps you lead those conversations with clarity and conviction.'

Debbie Wosskow OBE, Chair, Invest in Women Taskforce; non-executive Director, Channel 4

'A timely, practically packed bible for thinking about pricing and value systematically – and differently. It's relevant for a large corporate all the way to a solopreneur. The benefits flow directly to your bottom line.'

Sharath Jeevan OBE, author of Intrinsic *and* Inflection

'*The Pricing Sprint* helps teams move from opinion to insight and from debate to confident action. It's a thoughtful and genuinely useful guide for leaders who want pricing to work harder, without creating unnecessary disruption.'

Christoph Homann, CCO, Superstruct Entertainment

'This is gold. An utterly comprehensive and practical guide to the most challenging and high-stakes process in launching a new product or service. Establishing the value of what you're offering is a make-or-break moment and this book offers clear steps and nuanced insights into just how to get this right.'

Dave Jarman, Associate Professor in Innovation and Entrepreneurship, University of Bristol

'A jam-packed how-to of pricing, combining insight on behavioural psychology, economics, research, testing, design and customer communication.'

Richard Ambrose, CEO, Wealthify

'*The Pricing Sprint* gives founders and leadership teams a way to break out of the fear and the guesswork. It shows them how to uncover what customers really value, how to validate decisions before committing to them, and how to involve their whole organization in a process that builds confidence from the inside out.'

Polly Dhaliwal, COO, Enterprise Nation

'A must-read for any leader who wants pricing to drive growth. It's practical, insightful, and immediately actionable.'

Servaes Tholan, former CFO at Upwork and eBay North America

'The authors turn pricing into a hands-on design practice that uses research, prototyping, and iteration to create prices customers understand and value. This book is ideal for product, marketing, and service teams who want a practical guide to designing better prices.'

Marc Stickdorn, author of This is Service Design Thinking, *and* This is Service Design Doing

'*The Pricing Sprint* is the definitive guide to unlocking revenue through smarter pricing. If you are ready to stop guessing and start growing, this book is a game-changer.'

Maren Kunfermann, former CMO, ifolor

'Understanding how customers perceive value is an art that few truly master. This framework gives leaders like us a structured way to uncover that value and unlock the underlying growth potential.'

Adrien Salvat, CEO, Webinterpret

'This book gives you the ultimate pricing superpower! It is your not-so-secret weapon for driving customer growth for your organization. Whether you dip into it or read the whole manual end-to-end, it's your guide to becoming the pricing champion for your company.'

Nick Viney, CEO, Global App Testing

'*The Pricing Sprint* gives leaders in global, multi-segment businesses a practical framework to align teams, navigate legacy constraints, and make confident pricing decisions that actually stick.'

Tilda Molho, Digital & eCommerce Growth Leader, former Sky & eBay

'By providing concrete guidance on how to build and embed pricing capabilities within an organization, the book becomes not just a strategic resource but also a practical toolkit for long-term impact.'

Virpi Kaartti, PhD, Head of the Service Innovation and Design MBA, Laurea University of Applied Sciences

'*The Pricing Sprint* is a step-by-step guide that shows how to engage a team, gather evidence, make changes, and understand your positioning in the market. It provides an easy to follow blueprint – not just for a one-off pricing discussion, but for regular check-ins to ensure business objectives are being met and everyone is a part of the process. A must read for anyone in business.'

Rhea Freeman, business coach and mentor, author of You've Got This

'Pricing is one of those "dreaded topics" for most business owners, so we often avoid it. *The Pricing Sprint* demonstrates not only the power of pricing but how to get pricing right, with a simple step-by-step approach that takes the mystery and confusion out of it. By the end of this book, you'll know what a difference pricing can make, and how to start making it work for you.'

Ameesha Green, Founder & Director of Editorial, The Book Shelf

'*The Pricing Sprint* is a refreshing contribution to the field. It's a highly practical, down-to-earth look at what pricing really means, and how to make it work for your business.'

Dr Eve Poole OBE, author of Leadersmithing

'Too many leaders default to cost-plus pricing. This book shows that it is also a discipline grounded in empathy and experimentation and will completely change how you see pricing.'

Kaija Koivusalo, Senior Lecturer in Accounting,
Laurea University of Applied Sciences

THE PRICING SPRINT

12 Steps to Unlock the Power of Pricing

JENNY MILLAR AND ANN PADLEY

BLOOMSBURY BUSINESS

LONDON • NEW YORK • OXFORD • NEW DELHI • SYDNEY

BLOOMSBURY BUSINESS
Bloomsbury Publishing Plc, 50 Bedford Square, London, WC1B 3DP, UK
Bloomsbury Publishing Inc, 1359 Broadway, New York, NY 10018, USA
Bloomsbury Publishing Ireland Limited, 29 Earlsfort Terrace, Dublin 2, D02 AY28, Ireland

BLOOMSBURY, BLOOMSBURY BUSINESS and the Diana logo are trademarks of
Bloomsbury Publishing Plc

First published in Great Britain 2026

Cover design: Lisa Wright
Cover image: © Lisa Wright

Bloomsbury Publishing Plc does not have any control over, or responsibility for,
any third-party websites referred to or in this book. All internet addresses given in
this book were correct at the time of going to press. The authors and publisher regret
any inconvenience caused if addresses have changed or sites have ceased to exist,
but can accept no responsibility for any such changes.

A catalogue record for this book is available from the British Library.

A catalog record for this book is available from the Library of Congress.

ISBN: HB: 978-1-3994-3080-7
       ePDF: 978-1-3994-3081-4
       ePub: 978-1-3994-3083-8

Typeset by RefineCatch Limited, Bungay, Suffolk
Printed and bound in Great Britain

For product safety related questions contact productsafety@bloomsbury.com.

To find out more about our authors and books visit www.bloomsbury.com
and sign up for our newsletters

WELCOME

'These prices are killing me,' Jenny's eight-year-old muttered during a heated discussion about purchasing a new Pokémon card.

He was frustrated that the rarest cards cost the most, and frankly, it didn't feel fair. Jenny, of course, lit up because to her, this *was* pricing in action.

To a parent, Pokémon cards might seem like overpriced rectangles of laminated cardboard. But in a child's world, they're social currency – symbols of status, strategy and story.

It was the perfect reminder that value isn't rational. It's subjective and contextual.

Each year, we speak with hundreds of leaders about pricing and hear stories about the pricing changes they'd put off, the discomfort they felt, and the turning points that finally made them act. Through those conversations, we have heard pricing called a 'guessing game', 'black box', and even a 'dark art'.

Pricing sits at the uncomfortable intersection of money, value and human behaviour. It feels technical when it's anything but. Despite being one of the fastest ways to change the trajectory of a business, pricing is often sidelined, overlooked or driven by guesswork.

Pricing sits at the uncomfortable intersection of money, value and human behaviour.

We've seen companies leave millions on the table. Not because their product is wrong or their costs are too high, but because they've misjudged something far more complex: what people value.

That's why we wrote this book – to make sense of both the commercial and the human sides of pricing.

Our respective paths into pricing were different, yet complementary. Jenny's journey began in commercial leadership roles, chasing ambitious revenue targets without always having the right tools to deliver them. Pricing quickly became the lever she returned to, again and again. She was drawn to the challenge of finding the sweet spot between customer value, cost structure and commercial ambition. Over time, that curiosity became a calling.

Ann's career began in banking, where one jargon-filled bank statement too many convinced her there had to be a better way. Human-centred design and behavioural science offered the tools to decode how people make decisions and what they value most. Since then, she has worked with businesses around the world to redesign services that create better outcomes for people and the bottom line. After meeting Jenny, she became fascinated by pricing as a lens for what people truly value.

Together, we reimagined what pricing could look like when it started with people rather than products, and when commercial outcomes were driven by evidence, not instinct. What emerged was a practical and repeatable approach that equips teams to build pricing strategies with confidence and clarity. We call it The Pricing Sprint.

That approach has become the foundation for the work we do in our consultancy firm, Untapped Pricing. We built the business to reflect a simple belief that when pricing is approached with the right mix of evidence, empathy and experimentation, it has the power to do more than increase revenue. It can help teams work more confidently. It can shift how customers perceive value. And it can create momentum for growth in ways few other levers can.

This work has taken us to global stages, earned awards and, most importantly, helped teams unlock results they didn't think pricing could deliver. We've seen organizations transform financially *and* culturally when they stop treating pricing as a necessary evil and start seeing it as a strategic force for good.

You're holding the playbook we've spent years developing in the field, testing hypotheses, running experiments, coaching teams and learning what works (and what doesn't). If you're looking for a pricing guide that is clear-eyed, practical and designed to move quickly, this is for you.

Whether you're starting from uncertainty, obligation or ambition, we hope this book helps you use pricing as your most confident lever for growth.

Ann Padley and Jenny Millar

CONTENTS

Introduction:
The Pricing Sprint

Two companies raised their prices. One lost 18% of its customers. The other increased profit by 22%.

The first rushed through a blanket 10% uplift in a bid to 'fix margin'. The result was confusion, cancellations, loss of revenue and a sharp dip in morale for both customers and the internal team.

The second approached the challenge differently. They ran a Pricing Sprint, speaking to customers, identifying what mattered most, repackaging their offer, using testing to lower risk, and communicating with clarity. Their pricing uplift landed with confidence and delivered results that stuck.

Pricing, when mishandled, can quietly drain a business. When approached with the right evidence and intent, it becomes one of the most effective levers for growth.

From startups to multinational corporations, and not-for-profits to social enterprises, the 'price tag' decision underpins the viability of every organization. It determines whether they thrive or flounder, hire or fire, serve or cease.

Still, most leadership teams don't give pricing the attention it deserves until something forces their hand. Sometimes, it's rising costs and shrinking margins. Sometimes, it's the realization they haven't raised prices in years and the numbers no longer stack up. Sometimes, it's the desire to scale faster and the need to unlock more revenue to do it. The unfair advantage comes when teams start paying attention to pricing, whether it feels urgent or not.

Now, think about your organization. Is your pricing delivering the results you need?

If you're reading this, you likely suspect it could be working harder, but you're not sure where to begin or how to move from a gut feeling to a strategy that sticks.

The most effective teams start by asking questions:

- What matters most to your customers?
- Do you know what they truly value and what they're willing to pay for that value?
- Is your current pricing reinforcing your brand, or undermining it?

As you'll quickly see, these are deceptively simple questions with deeply complex answers.

Pricing isn't just a numbers game. The people on both sides of a price – the buyer and the seller – apply their own perspectives, preconceptions and emotions when setting or assessing prices. This adds a rich layer of subjectivity and complexity to unravel.

If you are uncertain about your pricing, are stuck in a reactive cycle, or are working from an outdated playbook, consider this:

- What if your 'price tag' could be used for more than just reacting to external pressures?

- What if pricing became an opportunity to deepen customer connections and shape your product positioning in a way that helps your business thrive?

- What if instead of fearing backlash about your price, it could inspire trust and communicate value to your customers?

If you are ready to turn pricing into your secret weapon for growth, this book is for you.

Pricing is both a commercial and behavioural challenge. It is part spreadsheet, part psychology, and doing it well means navigating both with clarity. You will learn how to take decisive pricing action, grounded in evidence and strategies that are good for your business and your customers.

Turn pricing into your secret weapon for growth.

The Pricing Sprint is a practical, 12-step process proven to transform your price, position and profitability.

We will show you how to bring together your existing data, team expertise and customer insights to rapidly build, test and refine your approach to pricing. The result is a pricing strategy that is customer-focused, market-aligned and built for growth – and a team that is engaged and ready to implement it.

The methodology you're about to learn has been honed and proven with organizations across the United Kingdom, the European Union and the United States. It's been used to price everything from beauty products, sports apparel and photo books to funeral services, business software and seismic technology. In this book, you'll find the process, tools and frameworks that have helped teams think critically about the value they deliver and align pricing with strategy. As one CEO recently described their Pricing Sprint: *"Articulating business value isn't rocket science, but combining this with pricing and using it to change people's mindset – this is unique. This is rocket science."*

We guide you and your team on a step-by-step journey through running your own Pricing Sprint, building clarity and confidence at each stage. It's called a sprint because it's designed for momentum. You are not racing through. You are concentrating your team's energy and attention on a series of critical pricing decisions and creating space for meaningful action by replacing endless debate with structured progress.

If you're a solopreneur or have a small team, you can still run a successful Pricing Sprint. While you may not have multiple team members to lean on, you can draw on external expertise, advisors or even trusted peers to provide input when you need it most.

You, your business and your team are unique. Your journey through your Pricing Sprint will be unique as well. Think of it as a 'choose your own adventure' experience. Some readers dip into the chapters most relevant to their situation to tackle an urgent challenge. Many work through it in sequence, building step by step to create a high-impact pricing strategy. Others run a series of focused sprints, each addressing a different aspect of pricing such as communicating value, testing psychological nudges or aligning pricing with strategic positioning.

The method is designed to run alongside day-to-day responsibilities, not replace them. Plan to take 4–12 weeks, depending on the type of sprint you run, whether that's short and focused or larger and more exploratory. Start by reading Chapters 1 and 2 for guidance on how to diagnose your biggest pricing opportunities and determine which kind of sprint is right for you. Whichever path

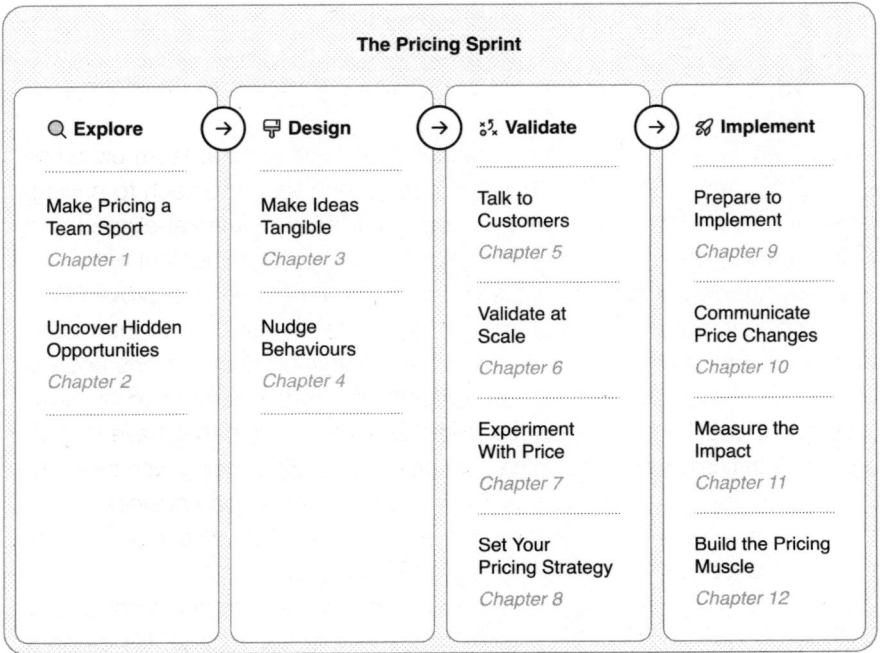

The Pricing Sprint

🔍 Explore	→	🖥 Design	→	⁝⁝ Validate	→	🖋 Implement
Make Pricing a Team Sport *Chapter 1*		Make Ideas Tangible *Chapter 3*		Talk to Customers *Chapter 5*		Prepare to Implement *Chapter 9*
Uncover Hidden Opportunities *Chapter 2*		Nudge Behaviours *Chapter 4*		Validate at Scale *Chapter 6*		Communicate Price Changes *Chapter 10*
				Experiment With Price *Chapter 7*		Measure the Impact *Chapter 11*
				Set Your Pricing Strategy *Chapter 8*		Build the Pricing Muscle *Chapter 12*

you take, the book will orient you to where you are now and where you could go next. The chapters are divided into four distinct phases:

Explore. You'll work to understand your current pricing reality: what's working, what's holding you back and where the biggest opportunities lie.

Design. You'll turn opportunities into tangible concepts, drawing inspiration from what's worked elsewhere, applying behavioural insights and shaping ideas that are worth testing.

Validate. You'll pressure-test your pricing decisions with customers and the broader market to reduce risk and increase confidence before finalizing your pricing strategy.

Implement. You'll focus on communicating and launching pricing changes with clarity, measuring the impact and building ongoing pricing capabilities.

As you work through your sprint, pricing shifts from a reactive task to a repeatable growth lever. You'll embed new ways of working and develop a proof of concept that builds the internal buy-in and investment that pricing deserves. Ultimately, you're doing much more than running a sprint. You're uncovering a strategic superpower that's been hiding in plain sight.

Are you ready to make pricing your most powerful growth lever? Let's dive in.

Explore

1

MAKE PRICING A TEAM SPORT

Like any great team sport, a Pricing Sprint is more effective and rewarding when everyone works together. Each player brings unique strengths to the field, whether it's setting the strategy, making key plays or supporting the team's overall effort. Along the way, there may be mistakes, but they become opportunities to regroup, refocus and improve. Most importantly, it's the collective effort and shared victories that create alignment and momentum for the next game.

Your Pricing Sprint is no different. By bringing key members of your team together, you not only share the workload but tap into diverse viewpoints, spark creativity and build alignment.

Dedicating a defined burst of activity that spreads across a number of weeks strikes a balance between speed and depth. It means your team stays focused and develops customer-focused strategies that are rigorously tested, market-aligned and primed for execution.

In this chapter, we'll guide you through the first steps to set your Pricing Sprint up for success. You'll learn how to assemble the right team, assess the current state of pricing and align everyone around shared goals and testable hypotheses.

Select Your Team

Let's start with the captain – likely, that's you.

If you feel like you've been handed the 'hot potato' of pricing, you're not alone. In many organizations, pricing lacks a clear home. It might be spread across teams like commercial, operations, finance, strategy or marketing or land on the founder or Chief of Staff. Often, pricing becomes a task no one fully owns, passed around because of its high stakes and complexity and the common underestimation of the resources it demands.

But here's the thing: if you've been handed this responsibility, you're in a powerful position to make a difference. With team collaboration and a learning mindset, you can thrive as a pricing leader, whether you're a reluctant hot-potato handler or an enthusiastic pricing aficionado. By assembling the right team and creating shared ownership, you'll build the foundation for meaningful improvements in your organization's long-term growth.

Assembling a cross-functional team ensures that you bring diverse perspectives and expertise to the table. The size and seniority of your team will vary depending on your business and available resources. Here are general guidelines you can adapt.

Form a Focused, Agile Team

Aim for a team of five to seven members to maintain diversity of thought while ensuring agility and focus.

- Larger teams can be harder to manage, often slowing progress with added bureaucracy. If you need to involve more than seven people, establish a core team and engage others as subject matter experts at key points.
- Smaller teams, while more agile, may lack the diversity of perspectives. If you are running your Pricing Sprint alone or with just one or two others, lean on trusted advisors or subject matter experts at critical stages to bring in fresh insights and challenge your assumptions.

Bring in Cross-Functional Voices

Your team should represent key areas such as sales, marketing, customer service, finance and product. Each role offers a unique point of view into a key aspect of the business.

- Sales, marketing, and customer service provide frontline insights into customer needs, objections and buying behaviour.
- Finance can provide access to key data, aid in analysis and forecasting, and be the voice for profitability and long-term financial sustainability.
- Product brings an understanding of production costs, innovation pipelines and product value.

Involve Senior Decision-Makers

Whenever possible, include senior leaders who are empowered to make swift decisions, help the process move forward efficiently, avoid unnecessary bottlenecks, and signal the importance of the Pricing Sprint to the rest of the organization. Senior leaders can help unlock access to key resources needed to execute the work while reserving their own time and expertise for high-level strategic input and making key decisions.

Set Clear Expectations

Set expectations early for a 'light touch' approach. Let your team know that their role is to provide insights and expertise without the process becoming overly time-consuming or burdensome. This helps keep everyone engaged while respecting their existing responsibilities.

Why pricing needs to be a team sport

Establishing a cross-functional team is more than theatrics. Pricing's influence extends deeply into every corner of your organization, influencing more than just the bottom line. How pricing, discounting and negotiation decisions are managed can have widespread and often unforeseen consequences. Decisions can cause ripple effects, both positive and negative, that permeate employee behaviours, operational dynamics and, ultimately, customer satisfaction and retention.

Pour & Prosper Coffee Co.* is a fiercely independent coffee brand known for its ethical sourcing, small-batch roasting and community focus. In addition to running local cafes, they also sell coffee beans online, distribute in bulk and provide coffee equipment and servicing. Let's look at a few areas where seemingly small pricing decisions may be causing ripple effects in their business.

A sales representative was tasked with selling coffee equipment to independent cafes. To hit their conversion targets and secure a year-end bonus, they continued to offer customers the maximum discounts available. While this approach boosted short-term sales metrics and won customer favour, it came at a significant cost to margins. Over time, what seemed like a well-meaning incentive ultimately undermined overall profitability.

Their UX designer was responsible for the coffee store's online website. A well-intentioned decision to showcase popular but low-cost coffee labels through prominent placement on the website led to an unintended outcome: even more customers gravitated towards the cheaper options, overlooking premium ones.

---

*Pour & Prosper Coffee Co. is a fictional business created to illustrate pricing concepts throughout this book. While the company is not real, the challenges, decisions and examples reflect real-world scenarios drawn from our experience. Any similarity in name to existing businesses is purely coincidental and unintended.

This shift affected revenue and led customers to perceive the brand as cost-conscious as opposed to high quality.

Finally, in an effort to offset rising costs, the CEO announced a price increase across all products. While the decision made financial sense on paper, it left the customer service team overwhelmed with complaints from retail and wholesale customers alike. Without proper alignment and support, the move damaged relationships and threatened long-term brand loyalty.

If a cross-functional team had collaborated from the start, these ripple effects could have been anticipated and mitigated. Instead of reacting to challenges after the fact, the team could have designed a strategy that balanced financial goals, customer expectations and operational realities. By aligning perspectives, the sales team might have refined discounting policies, the UX team could have highlighted premium offerings, and the CEO's price increase might have been supported by effective customer communication.

Pricing isn't just a financial lever; it's a mechanism to steer customer perceptions, shape employee behaviours and drive organizational culture. Involving cross-functional teams ensures that pricing decisions reflect a holistic understanding of the business, helping to align strategies with organizational goals and minimize unintended consequences.

Assess the Current State

Now that your team is assembled, the next step is to gain a clear understanding of your current pricing practices. Think of this as taking a snapshot of where you stand today. By identifying strengths and weaknesses upfront, you can focus your efforts where they'll have the most impact.

This step doesn't require lengthy analysis or perfect answers, and speed and honesty are key. A quick yes/no survey can help your team hone in on areas of pricing that may need attention. The goal isn't to fix everything immediately but to establish a baseline and prioritize the most critical opportunities for improvement.

To guide this assessment, use the Pricing Appraisal Scorecard (Figure 1.1). This scorecard is divided into four categories: pricing management, pricing psychology, pricing strategy and pricing confidence. Each is designed to highlight specific aspects of your pricing practices. Remember, a simple yes or no response is all you need. Move quickly, relying on your existing knowledge and observations.

Pricing Appraisal Scorecard	
Pricing Management	**Yes/No**
1. Is there a clear internal owner for all pricing decisions?	
2. Do you experiment with pricing?	
3. Can you measure the financial impact of price changes and discounts?	
4. Do you track which products/services are most profitable?	
5. Are customer-facing team members comfortable talking about prices?	
Pricing Psychology	**Yes/No**
6. Can your prices be understood in under 10 seconds?	
7. Do you typically give customers options to choose from?	
8. Are prices typically accompanied by a clear statement of value?	
9. Do you signpost customers to the best choice(s) for them?	
10. Does your pricing tell the same story as your brand?	
Pricing Strategy	**Yes/No**
11. Do you regularly review your pricing strategy?	
12. Is your business profitable enough to achieve your goals?	
13. Do prices change when you extend or enhance your offering?	
14. Have you validated how much customers are willing to pay?	
15. Do you know what customers consider to be their alternatives?	
Pricing Confidence	**Yes/No**
16. Are you certain you're not leaving money on the table?	
17. Do you get feedback from customers before changing prices?	
18. Do you know when customers don't buy because of price?	
19. Can your team consistently describe your approach to pricing?	
20. Do you feel confident making pricing decisions?	

Figure 1.1 Pricing Appraisal Scorecard.

Once you've completed the scorecard, take a moment to collate responses from across the team and reflect on any patterns.

- If most responses to a question are 'no', this may signal a gap in your pricing practices. These are likely areas that have been overlooked or underoptimized and offer clear opportunities for improvement.

- If most responses are 'yes', these are areas where your organization is performing well. Acknowledge what's working and continue to build on this strong foundation.

- Mixed responses may reveal differences in expectations or understanding within the team. These are worth exploring together to find out what's dividing opinion.

Whatever patterns emerge, this appraisal gives you a clear starting point. By assessing your current state, you've laid the foundation for a more confident and strategic approach to pricing. As you continue your Pricing Sprint, you will build on these insights to drive meaningful improvements and align your organization for pricing success.

Draft a Blueprint

With a quick assessment under your belt, your next step is to capture a snapshot of what your pricing strategy is now. Many teams rush into solution mode, but without this shared picture of what pricing looks like today and why, it's difficult to make informed decisions. Taking the time to document where you are today offers two key benefits:

1. It unites your team, surfaces differing perspectives, and spotlights areas of tension.
2. It provides a clear baseline, making it easier to identify gaps and opportunities.

We have developed a tool called the Pricing Strategy Blueprint to help teams visualize their existing pricing strategy at the outset of their sprint and crystallize the desired future they are working towards. It offers a single-page snapshot of where you are, where you are going and what that shift means in practice.

Use the left-hand side of your blueprint to draft the current state of your pricing. Some elements may be straightforward to complete, while others might feel like complete unknowns. For prompts you can't answer, reach out to others in your organization to gather the information you need. Once your draft is

	Current	Future
North Star Goal *What are we optimizing pricing for?*	*Example* Acquisition: We are focused on rapidly gaining market share	*Example* Retention: We want to build long-term relationships with customers
Brand Position *What does our price say about our brand?*		
Pricing Model *How do we charge?*		
Price Setting *How do we set our prices?*		
Price Changes *How & when do we change prices?*		
Discounts *How & when do we discount?*		
Pricing Process *How are pricing decisions made & by whom?*		
Pricing Measurements *How do we measure performance?*		
Pricing Psychology *What behaviours do we nudge?*		

Figure 1.2 Pricing Strategy Blueprint.

complete, review it with your Pricing Sprint team. This step is critical, as different team members may understand the current strategy differently. Iterate the draft until you feel confident that you've captured the current state of pricing as accurately as possible.

Don't worry if things feel murky. We often work with teams where the logic behind current pricing is unclear, or lost over time as people move on or decisions go undocumented. This is exactly why creating a shared view now is so valuable. You're not just mapping what is, but laying the groundwork for what comes next.

Next, it's time to use the right-hand side to draft the future state of your pricing. This step follows a similar process to the one you used for the current state, just with a forward-looking lens.

At this stage, nothing is set in stone. The goal isn't to define a perfect end state but to start categorizing areas based on what you know now. As you work through each prompt, use three action types to categorize your thinking:

1. **Pivot.** This is the low-hanging fruit; in other words, areas where you or the team see immediate opportunities for change. For example, if no one is currently accountable for pricing decisions, you can establish clarity and ownership right away.

2. **Maintain.** These are areas where the current state is working well and should remain as is. This category helps you recognize what's already strong and avoid fixing things that aren't broken.

3. **Explore.** These are areas where change is needed but the path forward isn't clear yet. You'll rely on research, data and experimentation to determine the right approach. These are ideal areas to focus on during your Pricing Sprint as they are ripe for making meaningful progress towards actionable solutions.

Remember, the future state is a working draft based on current assumptions, so stay flexible and open to changes as you gather new evidence and insights. The goal isn't to create a perfect plan right away but to establish a strong foundation for making confident, informed decisions about pricing.

Completing this one-page view can be revealing. For seasoned team members, it often sharpens awareness of where the current approach is working or falling short. For newcomers, it offers a quick, coherent understanding of past decisions. For everyone, it connects pricing to your broader business goals and provides a shared framework for future decisions.

Chart Your Destination

Pricing can be used very deliberately to drive revenue or margin or volume, but rarely all three at the same time. Being clear about what you want to achieve ensures that your pricing decisions contribute directly to your goals.

Let's stress-test the North Star Goal you have already drafted in the future state of your Pricing Strategy Blueprint. Review what you wrote and ask two simple questions:

- Is this the number one goal our pricing strategy should be optimizing for?
- Is this goal aligned to our broader business priorities?

If you can answer a confident yes to both questions, you've landed on a compelling North Star and your stress test is complete. If you answered no, work with your team to refine your North Star Goal.

Getting this goal right is pivotal to the success of your Pricing Sprint. You'll return to it frequently to stress-test your direction of travel as you validate and refine your pricing strategy. For example, if your North Star Goal is to grow market share, a strategy focused on lower prices and frequent discounts makes strategic sense as it helps attract price-sensitive customers and rapidly expand your base. However, if your priority is to maximize profit, that same approach should raise a red flag, as aggressive discounting could erode margins and attract the wrong customers. In this case, your team may re-evaluate the data and realise that higher prices with minimal discounting focused on your most valuable segments would better support long-term profitability, even if it means serving fewer customers overall.

For one European gift retailer, the goal-setting process surfaced tensions among the leadership team and its board members. Some members of the team felt the pressure from competitors and wanted to focus on defending and growing their dominant market share. Others were mindful of feedback from loyal customers that their product quality and service were differentiators in the market. They wanted to focus on capturing the headroom on price after years of pricing conservatively. Achieving growth in market share demanded a pricing strategy that was entirely different to one aimed at driving revenue or profitability. Meaningful progress with pricing could only begin once the team aligned on a clear objective.

North Star Goal	Potential Pricing Strategy	Possible Trade-Off
Increase market share	• Lower prices • Widespread promotions	Decreased revenue or gross profit
Increase revenue	• Competitive prices • Targeted promotions to drive specific high-value purchase behaviours	Volume decrease
Increase profitability	• Value-based pricing • Raise prices above the competition where possible • Use discounts sparingly	Volume decrease

Figure 1.3 Potential pricing strategies for a European gift retailer.

Schedule Stops Along the Way

Optimizing your pricing doesn't have to feel like an endless marathon. Instead, think of it as a series of manageable Pricing Sprints: focused, strategic bursts of activity that drive progress. Each Pricing Sprint is designed to help you tackle a specific aspect of pricing, giving you clear outcomes and actionable insights without overwhelming your team.

Pricing Sprints provide the structure to test ideas, gather feedback and adapt based on what you learn. Rather than aiming for a set-it-and-forget-it approach, this iterative process allows you to refine your strategy as you go, ensuring that each step is informed by data, customer insights and practical experience. The result? A more effective and responsive pricing model that evolves with your business.

Not all Pricing Sprints will look the same. Some may have a clear focus and outcome from the start while others may be more exploratory. Here are two examples of Pricing Sprints we might run at Untapped Pricing to illustrate the range of possibilities.

A Short and Focused Pricing Sprint

Imagine that your Pricing Appraisal Scorecard revealed consistent gaps in pricing psychology. Your goal might not be to overhaul pricing but to better understand how customers perceive and engage with your prices throughout the purchase journey. You could plan a short, focused Pricing Sprint lasting 4 weeks or less.

You might start by reviewing your pricing journey through the lens of psychological nudges (see Chapter 4). Are your price points clearly signalling value? Is the customer presented with options that nudge them towards higher-value choices? Are they presented with choices at all? Then, you could conduct five targeted interviews with customers (see Chapter 5) to uncover how they experience your pricing in the context of their buying decisions. Finally, based on what you learn, you could make small adjustments to your pricing presentation (see Chapter 4) and run a live experiment (see Chapter 6) to test the impact of these changes.

In this case, your Pricing Sprint will focus on small, incremental adjustments that are quick to implement and easy to measure. The outcome is actionable insights and immediate results without requiring significant time or resources.

A Larger, Exploratory Pricing Sprint

If your Pricing Appraisal Scorecard revealed gaps across the four categories of pricing – management, psychology, strategy and confidence – a more comprehensive Pricing Sprint may be the best approach. Spanning 10–12 weeks, this type of Pricing Sprint allows your team to follow a more structured journey through the chapters of this book, addressing foundational issues and uncovering opportunities for meaningful transformation.

Start by gathering input from across your team to build a clear picture of your current pricing landscape. This exploration phase can surface misalignments, highlight areas of friction and reveal potential quick wins. From there, you can prioritize your efforts, focusing on the most impactful opportunities (Chapter 2).

As the Pricing Sprint progresses, you'll explore key areas like understanding customer perceptions of value (Chapters 5 and 6), start experimenting with changes (Chapters 3, 4 and 7) and refine your pricing strategy to better align with your business goals (Chapter 8). Throughout this process, your team will rely on iterative testing and evidence-based decision-making to refine your approach.

By the end of this larger Pricing Sprint, your pricing strategy will be clearer, more cohesive, and grounded in data and insights. You will also have built the internal capability (Chapters 9–12) to approach pricing with confidence and agility, both now and in the future.

As you move through your Pricing Sprint, you may find that priorities shift or new insights emerge. It's all part of the process. Continue to think of this journey as a 'choose your own adventure' experience. You may decide to dig deep into certain areas, skim over others, or revisit steps as your understanding grows.

Adopt the Right Mindsets

Along the way, challenge yourself and your team to adopt two key design thinking mindsets: progress over perfection and learning over being right.

By prioritizing progress over perfection, you can maintain focus and keep moving forward rather than getting caught up in having to get everything exactly right. This mindset encourages you to test ideas and progress quickly, embracing the idea even small steps can lead to significant breakthroughs.

Adopt two key design thinking mindsets: progress over perfection and learning over being right.

Similarly, embracing learning over being right shifts the focus from defending assumptions to uncovering what truly works. This mindset fosters curiosity, encourages experimentation, and invites a willingness to adapt based on evidence and feedback. Keep an open mind and you're bound to encounter insights that challenge your initial beliefs – in the best possible way!

No two Pricing Sprints will look exactly the same, and these mindsets enable you to stay flexible and resilient, making the most of the unique opportunities your journey presents. It's this adaptability that makes a Pricing Sprint so powerful.

Take a moment to think about what you want to achieve with your first Pricing Sprint, map out your steps, and prepare to bring your team along for the ride.

Turn Opinions into Hypotheses

Before you dive into the next step of your Pricing Sprint, it's worth addressing one of the trickiest dynamics you're likely to encounter: differing opinions within your team. Just like in any great team sport, these differences can either slow you down or push you forward, depending on how you manage them. Let's take a moment to explore how to turn these debates into opportunities for breakthrough thinking.

When you bring together perspectives from across the business, debates and disagreements are inevitable. Contrasting views and differing motivations will emerge, and while these conflicting opinions often tend to cloud judgment and stall progress, they can also hold the potential to unlock valuable insights.

Let's think back to Pour & Prosper Coffee Co. The sales veteran might push for competitive undercutting to close deals faster. The CFO might advocate for premium pricing to protect profitability and strengthen the brand's positioning. Marketing might argue for a more segmented approach tailored to customers' differing willingness to pay. While these viewpoints may initially seem at odds, they each represent unique vantage points that can sharpen your pricing strategy.

Whether you're leading your Pricing Sprint team or contributing as a member, your goal is not to quell dissent or homogenize thought. Instead, embrace the mindset of learning over being right and transform individual convictions into opportunities for collective learning by reframing them as testable hypotheses. For example, the earlier perspectives might become hypotheses to validate such as:

- A lower introductory price will drive increased sales volume.
- Our brand's positioning adds measurable value that supports premium pricing.
- Regular customers are willing to pay 15% more than occasional buyers.

These statements will form the basis for the upcoming stages of your Pricing Sprint, where you'll gather evidence through research (Chapters 5 and 6) and experimentation (Chapter 7), ultimately using that evidence to set your pricing strategy (Chapter 8). This approach channels differing perspectives into a unified process of discovery, where evidence, rather than gut feelings, guides decision-making.

Just like in team sports, where missteps and disagreements are part of the game, these moments of friction can lead to breakthroughs when managed constructively. By capturing and testing these diverse ideas as part of your Pricing Sprint, you not only strengthen your strategy but also build a stronger, more cohesive team who are ready to tackle future challenges together.

Plan Your Next Step

Step one is now complete, and you've just laid the groundwork for meaningful progress. You've assembled a cross-functional team, mapped out the current state of your pricing, set clear goals for what pricing needs to achieve, identified areas for deeper exploration, and adopted a mindset that transforms differing opinions into testable hypotheses. Together, these elements form a strong foundation for the work ahead.

Now, it's time to build on that foundation. In the next chapter, you'll discover how to uncover the insights hidden within your organization by examining internal processes, customer sentiment, competitor pricing and internal data. This step focuses on identifying quick wins and uncovering the patterns and drivers of profitability, sparking the 'aha!' moments that will drive your Pricing Sprint forward with clarity and purpose.

PRICING PLAYBOOK: MAKE PRICING A TEAM SPORT

Here are your first five steps to get your Pricing Sprint underway:

1. **Select your team**
   Build a small, cross-functional team (five to seven people) with input from sales, product, finance, marketing and customer support.

2. **Assess the current state of pricing**
   Use the Pricing Appraisal Scorecard with your team to quickly identify strengths, gaps and misalignments.

3. **Agree your North Star**
   Align with your team on what pricing needs to deliver. Is it more customers, higher revenue or stronger margins? Pick one and let it guide every decision.

4. **Outline your Pricing Sprint plan**

   Decide whether you'll run a short, focused sprint or a deeper, exploratory one. Map the chapters you'll work through and set aside time in your calendars.

5. **Turn opinions into hypotheses**

   Reframe strong opinions as testable statements you can validate through research and experimentation.

2
UNCOVER HIDDEN OPPORTUNITIES

Understanding what truly drives or limits profitability within your organization is the next step in collecting the evidence to inform your pricing decisions.

In this chapter, we'll explore four key areas where you can look for insights into your organization's profitability drivers and inhibitors:

1. **Internal process.** How do existing processes and practices impact pricing?

2. **Customer sentiment.** What signals are customers and prospects sending that give insight into how they perceive your current pricing?

3. **Competitor pricing.** What information do you have about how competitors price?

4. **Internal data.** What does financial and behavioural data reveal about existing pockets of growth and profitability?

The goal of this exploration is to uncover those 'aha!' insights where clues in your existing data reveal unexpected but powerful realizations that spark a breakthrough in the way the team thinks on a strategic level. That collective 'aha!' means you've hit on insights that can help you and your team identify and prioritize a range of opportunities for pricing from quick wins to longer-term gains. This prioritization then becomes your roadmap for where to focus the efforts of your first and subsequent Pricing Sprints.

Think of this process as a fishing expedition. You have your boat, bait and a map of the lake. Sometimes, you might get lucky and find a school of fish immediately. Other times, you may need to cast your line repeatedly, trying different areas before you reel in the big catch. The key is persistence, planning, and the willingness to adapt based on what you find beneath the surface. Just as a seasoned angler knows when to change bait or move to a new location, you'll need to adjust your approach based on the insights you gather, ensuring that you're fishing where the big fish are likely to be.

By systematically exploring and sharing learnings, you'll equip your Pricing Sprint team with the knowledge and confidence to make data-driven pricing decisions that drive profitability and align with your broader business goals.

Map Your Pricing Process

Looking at the end-to-end process your internal teams follow can reveal unexpected insights. Often, each team member focuses solely on their specific part of the pricing process, making it easy to lose sight of how individual decisions influence overall profitability. However, when your team takes a step back and views the process holistically, it can reveal opportunities for significant profit improvement that might otherwise be overlooked.

After the team at Pour & Prosper Coffee Co. closed a deal, three colleagues sat around the table discussing how the pricing for that deal had been determined.

The sales manager said, 'We set the price to undercut the competition and win the deal quickly.'

The CFO replied, 'I assumed the price aligned with our standard margin requirements.'

The product manager argued, 'I thought the price we set reflected the added value of the custom features we delivered.'

Notice the misalignment? Now ask yourself: How well would your team align if asked a similar question about your last pricing decision?

This simple exercise highlights why mapping your pricing process as a team is so valuable. By creating a shared understanding across departments, you can reduce blind spots, uncover inefficiencies, and make smarter, more consistent decisions that drive profitability.

To do this, we create a Pricing Process Map. A Pricing Process Map is a simple, visual summary of the steps your team takes that are connected to pricing (directly or indirectly), starting with getting a lead in the door through to billing and ongoing support. Figure 2.1 provides an example of this for an enterprise technology provider. It illustrates how pricing decisions are influenced by multiple teams, from sales and delivery to finance and accounting, across key stages such as discovery, proposal creation, negotiation and project delivery. It highlights not only where pricing is set, but where it is shaped, challenged and, ultimately, reinforced through operational handovers.

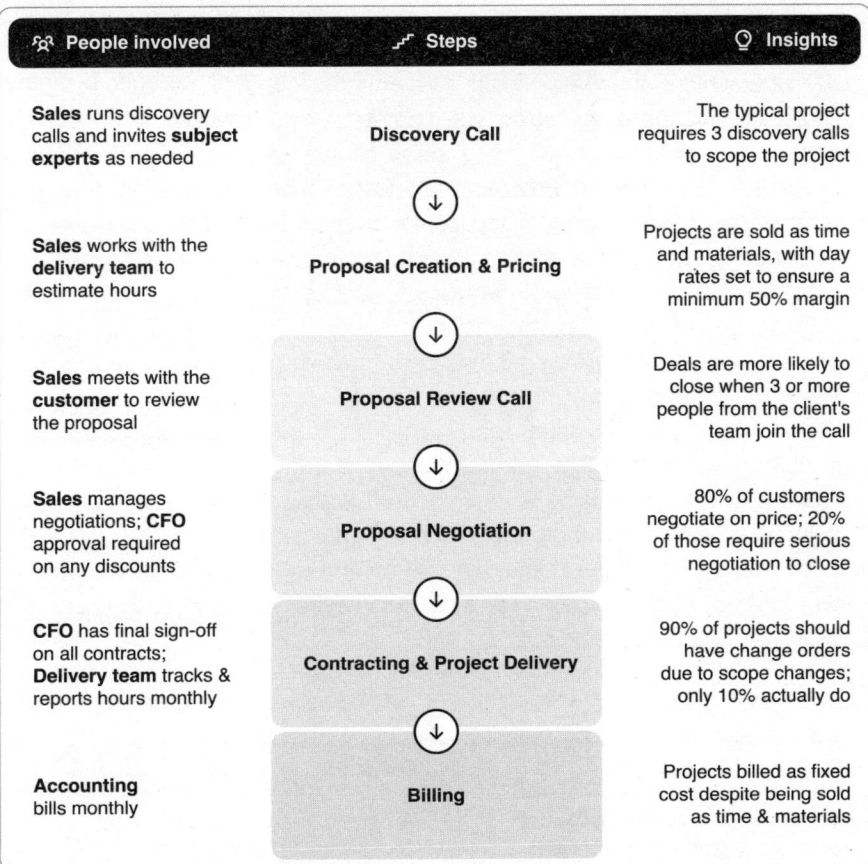

👥 People involved	🛤 Steps	💡 Insights
Sales runs discovery calls and invites **subject experts** as needed	**Discovery Call**	The typical project requires 3 discovery calls to scope the project
Sales works with the **delivery team** to estimate hours	**Proposal Creation & Pricing**	Projects are sold as time and materials, with day rates set to ensure a minimum 50% margin
Sales meets with the **customer** to review the proposal	**Proposal Review Call**	Deals are more likely to close when 3 or more people from the client's team join the call
Sales manages negotiations; **CFO** approval required on any discounts	**Proposal Negotiation**	80% of customers negotiate on price; 20% of those require serious negotiation to close
CFO has final sign-off on all contracts; **Delivery team** tracks & reports hours monthly	**Contracting & Project Delivery**	90% of projects should have change orders due to scope changes; only 10% actually do
Accounting bills monthly	**Billing**	Projects billed as fixed cost despite being sold as time & materials

Figure 2.1 Simple Pricing Process Map for an enterprise technology provider.

By creating your own Pricing Process Map, you will:

- Capture the as-is state of how pricing strategy is managed across the business.
- Reveal the alignment, or lack thereof, between various departments.
- Uncover potential bottlenecks, inefficiencies and strengths within your pricing process.
- Build a shared view of how each person's role helps put your pricing into practice.

A great starting point for creating your map is to interview four to five people in your business who represent a range of roles, from the initial sale through to final billing. These may be members of your sprint team or others in the business who can provide insight into a specific step in the process. Use the questions in Figure 2.2 to guide your discussions and pay close attention to the patterns and gaps that emerge in their responses.

By conducting these interviews, you'll gather comprehensive insights into the internal pricing process, highlighting areas of strength and opportunities for improvement. Your Pricing Process Map will provide new visibility into your current pricing process, surfacing critical focus areas for your Pricing Sprint and identifying early 'quick wins' that can build momentum. These quick wins might include streamlining inefficient workflows, addressing small but impactful misalignments between departments, or uncovering low-hanging fruit that can immediately boost profitability, such as better tracking of project hours or more consistent application of pricing policies.

Beyond its immediate value, the Pricing Process Map can also become a powerful tool for onboarding new team members. It gives them a clear, visual representation of how pricing is implemented across the organization, helping them quickly understand their role within the broader process. Over time, the map also serves as a living document that can be revisited and refined as your pricing strategy evolves, making it an ongoing asset for driving alignment and continuous improvement.

Ask	Listen for
What questions do customers or prospects commonly ask about pricing?	Where confusion, sensitivity and expectations show up in the buying journey
How do you currently set prices?	The current pricing model being used and consistency of the approach
Where do pricing conversations get difficult?	Common objections, negotiation patterns or areas of customer resistance
Which types of customers, products or projects tend to be more profitable?	Signals that point to pricing power, clear value or efficiency
How do you currently track and assess profitability?	The reports and data that are available to support pricing decisions
Where does profitability get squeezed or eroded?	Situations where pricing doesn't reflect cost, value or effort required
What external or internal factors make pricing more difficult?	Dependencies, constraints or broader business issues that influence pricing decisions

Figure 2.2 Pricing Process Map interview questions.

Why mapping your pricing process matters

Our team uses the Pricing Process Map as a tool to create a snapshot of how a company is implementing its pricing strategy across the organization. Creating the map is just the beginning. Reviewing it as a team often sparks the biggest 'aha!' moments, uncovering inefficiencies, misalignments and untapped opportunities. Here are the stories of two clients and the transformative insights that their internal Pricing Process Map revealed.

The software company and the disappearing margins

At first glance, Infomentum (a UK-based technology company) seemed to have everything under control. The sales team prided itself on its ability to respond quickly to customer needs, delivering tailored proposals that were sharp, professional and fast. Customer satisfaction was outstanding.

But cracks emerged when we mapped their internal pricing process. The development team responsible for delivering the work wasn't involved in creating estimates. Instead, they were handed numbers with no input – a frustration that later came to light.

> 'After reviewing the internal pricing process map as a team, I realized that our Head of Product Delivery has been upset for some time about not being involved in the estimations. A lot of these estimations were done and given to his team to manage, but he had no input in them whatsoever,' the CTO shared.

The development team revealed another issue:

> 'We're not tracking hours consistently. When we do, sometimes we shift actual hours worked into different parts of the project just to align with the original estimate.'

While these adjustments were made to avoid disruptions, they left the sales team without accurate data to improve future estimates. As one team member explained, 'If we miss out 50 or 100 hours across every project, it has a huge knock-on effect.'

The billing department added another layer to the story. Although projects were sold as time-and-materials, they were often billed as flat fees. And because change orders were rarely requested, even when project scopes expanded, margins took a hit.

By mapping the internal pricing process, the team uncovered four key insights:

1. Change orders are underutilized, yet they have the potential to impact project margin by 10-15%.
2. Time-and-materials projects are being billed at a flat fee impacting profit margin by another 10%.
3. Lack of accurate tracking left sales unable to improve future estimates.
4. Excluding the development team from the estimation process created gaps that rippled through the project lifecycle.

The map became a turning point. By involving the development team in scoping, tracking hours accurately and getting change orders and billing under control, the company began recovering lost margins and improving collaboration across teams. That's even before they looked at changing a single price.

The technology company and the target price loophole

Meanwhile, we were working with a sensor technology company. Like Infomentum, they appeared to have a well-structured approach to pricing. They had a global sales team, and their detailed pricing calculator ensured accuracy and consistency across geographies. Finance had carefully calculated a minimum price to protect margins and there was a clear process in place for how and when the sales team could offer discounts. The pricing calculator included a target price, intended to signal to the sales team the price they should aim for.

On the surface, the system appeared seamless.

We brought the team together in a Zoom call to walk through the process step by step. Everything seemed straightforward, until we reached the target price. That's when an uncomfortable question surfaced.

'Wait, who actually sets the target price?' someone asked.

The answer was no one. Finance thought the Chief Commercial Officer (CCO) had been actively managing the target price. The CCO thought finance was.

While the carefully planned pricing calculator provided useful guardrails, there was no assigned ownership for proactively managing the target price. Instead, it was being left to an outdated formula in a spreadsheet and was quietly eroding margins.

For the CCO, the insight was striking: *'The most powerful moment of the Pricing Sprint for me was realizing that no one was actively managing the target price!'*

This simple discovery had an outsized impact. By assigning responsibility for target price approval, the company restored its margins and ensured accountability moving forward.

Together, these two examples highlight the power of mapping the internal pricing process. Whether it's uncovering inefficiencies like missing hours and underutilized change orders or clarifying accountability for key pricing decisions, this process reveals the hidden dynamics that quietly impact profitability.

Explore Customer Sentiment

The next place to look for insights into your existing pricing is customer and prospective customer feedback. You may find feedback from customers about price in satisfaction surveys, anecdotally through remarks on social media, or documented by your sales representatives.

Chances are, on the surface the feedback about price contains a raft of grumbles and complaints. Dig a bit further and you may even find that your most satisfied customers say they would prefer to pay less. However, complaining about price is a low-hanging fruit for customers and prospects as it's an accessible and straightforward grievance that people can easily articulate. This tendency means that feedback on pricing can be disproportionately negative and not always reflective of the overall value or satisfaction that your product or service provides. Negative feedback about price is easy prey; it doesn't always equate to a genuine need for pricing adjustments.

Negative feedback about price is easy prey; it doesn't always equate to a genuine need for pricing adjustments.

As part of a Pricing Sprint team, you'll need to navigate the challenge of negativity bias, a common psychological trap where we disproportionately focus on critical feedback. When a handful of negative comments about pricing loom large in your decision-making, they can foster a culture of caution rather than decisive action. This can hold your team back from implementing new strategies or raising prices due to fear of backlash from customers.

To overcome this, ensure that you consider the full range of data you have available when making strategic pricing decisions. Better yet, go out and talk to your customers directly (we'll show you how in Chapter 4) to understand their perspective on price. By broadening your perspective, you can move past fear-driven reactions and towards confident, evidence-backed pricing decisions.

When analysing customer feedback data, watch for these key signals:

- **Red herrings: Misleading statistics or comments on price that mask the real story.**
  For example, a few customers complain your product is 'too expensive', but deeper analysis reveals their budgets fall far below your target market's average, making their feedback irrelevant to your pricing strategy.

- **Pricing hypocrisy: When customer behaviour contradicts their complaints about price.**
  For instance, a customer negotiates aggressively for a discount but then adds premium features or upgrades at full price.

- **The quiet steal: When silence speaks volumes.**
  If customers never question the price, especially for a consistently sold-out top-tier product, it may be a sign that you're underpricing.

Why price complaints don't always mean you are too expensive

Just because customers mention price doesn't mean it's a real problem. Without context, it's easy to misdiagnose. Let's see what this could look like in practice.

Pour & Prosper Coffee Co.'s marketing team were poring over results from the annual satisfaction survey. One data point leaps out: fifty respondents mentioned that prices are too high, and the feedback feels damning. The instinct might be to sound the alarm – clearly, price is a problem.

But digging deeper revealed a very different story. The survey received 5,000 responses, meaning those fifty complaints represent just 1% of the total feedback. That leaves 99% of respondents who didn't mention price at all. Suddenly, the 'pricing problem' seemed much smaller.

Then comes another twist: the 1% of respondents who did mention price were actually among the most satisfied customers overall. This added context reframes the complaints as a **red herring**, a misleading signal that distracts from the broader truth. Rather than indicating a pricing crisis, these comments suggest that prices might be nearing the upper limit of willingness-to-pay for this small group, but they haven't exceeded it.

Even more telling, those who expressed dissatisfaction with pricing still went on to make purchases or even upgrades. This is a clear case of **pricing hypocrisy**, where vocal objections to price don't match customer actions.

And then there's another intriguing insight. Among a different segment of highly satisfied buyers, there wasn't a single mention of price. This silence could point to a **quiet steal**, a situation where a lack of price pushback suggests that customers perceive exceptional value. These customers may see the price as so fair, or even low, that they don't feel the need to comment, potentially signalling that the product or service might be underpriced.

Pinning problems on price can be deceptively easy. It's a convenient scapegoat when dissatisfaction could stem from a range of other issues. As this scenario shows, context is everything. By zooming out and examining the full picture, you can uncover hidden dynamics such as red herrings, pricing hypocrisy and quiet steals.

Benchmark the Competition

The next place to look is your competitors. Competitor price benchmarking can offer valuable insights into market positioning, customer expectations and potential pricing opportunities or threats. Understanding this competitive landscape is an important piece of the puzzle to get the full picture of a range of pricing opportunities.

For companies just starting with competitor benchmarking, how you approach it will depend largely on how transparent your competitors are with their pricing.

If your competitors publish pricing, start by conducting a manual scrape of competitor websites to collect pricing data, especially if you have a small number of key competitors. For more comprehensive coverage or a large volume of products, consider using price-scraping tools to automate the process and track changes over time. These tools help you stay updated with the latest pricing strategies that your competitors are employing.

For a large number of products or categories, be intentional about which products are most critical to compare. Prioritize comparisons of Known Value Indicator (KVI) products. These are products with high price visibility where even small changes can influence how customers perceive your entire pricing strategy. Staying on the pulse of increases or decreases in these items offers a valuable signal of how your business is keeping pace with the broader market.

If your competitors don't publish pricing, begin by tapping into anecdotal data from your sales teams. Salespeople often gather valuable insights during their conversations with customers and prospects, learning what competitors are charging and how those prices influence customer decisions. This data, while informal, can be a valuable starting point. Additionally, you can leverage industry reports and insights from trusted advisors, such as board members or others in the business with experience in different companies, who might have tacit knowledge about competitor pricing strategies.

If you have competitor benchmarking practices in place, spend time reflecting on the data you have in order to draw additional insights. Here are some things to look out for:

- **Frequency of pricing changes.** Assess how often your competitors adjust their pricing and compare this to your frequency of benchmarking. Regular updates ensure that you are not working with outdated information.

- **Product comparisons.** Determine what proportion of your products/ services are exact matches, like-for-like comparisons or radically different offerings. This helps in making more accurate pricing decisions based on relevant data.

- **Competitor selection.** Re-evaluate which competitors you are benchmarking against and how direct the comparisons are. Ensure the competitors you focus on are those your customers actually consider (see Chapters 5 and 6 for how to validate this).

- **Coverage.** Identify any competition that isn't represented in your current benchmarking. This could include indirect competitors or alternatives that customers might consider, such as doing the work in-house or opting for a simpler solution in the case of service businesses.

Why do competitor price benchmarking

Sometimes, competitor price benchmarking reveals a hard truth that you can't ignore.

That's exactly what happened to Numan, a UK-based digital health brand that was operating in a fiercely competitive market. Price wars were rampant, and the team assumed they were simply keeping pace with the downward trend. But when we dived into their price-comparison data alongside internal analysis, the reality hit them: they weren't just keeping pace, they were leading the race to the bottom.

Without realizing it, their pricing decisions were driving an industry-wide price war. This insight forced a strategic pivot. By systematically testing higher prices, they were able to reposition their brand, increase profitability, and create more flexibility for future promotions. Competitor benchmarking showed them where they stood in the market and gave them the clarity to take back control of their strategy.

As you conduct your own benchmarking against the competition, use caution not to let your findings or your strategy be dictated entirely by competitors. In the case of Numan, competitor benchmarking held the final key to a powerful pricing insight. However, that insight was only realized within the wider context of their position as a market leader.

Being driven by the competition often works well for commodity products like milk or petrol and services like energy and internet access that are undifferentiated from the competition, particularly when it is known that customers shop around and make price-led decisions. It can also be effective in markets where availability drives value, such as semiconductors. In these cases, suppliers holding greater stock during times of scarcity can command a premium, even if the products themselves are not highly differentiated.

For innovative businesses or those with a distinct proposition, however, competitor-led pricing is often misapplied. Even when they offer clear differentiation, many still default to competitor benchmarks. This tendency is understandable: competitor data feels concrete, familiar and readily available, especially compared to the more involved work of uncovering customer perceptions of value. However, relying on competitors as your primary reference point brings significant risks.

First, competitor-led pricing puts competitors in the driving seat of your pricing strategy. Letting other organizations dictate how you set prices is highly reactive and hands over control to competing companies. At best, you may be leaving money on the table. At worst, this strategy may spark an unsustainable price war if competitors are adopting the same approach. This can lead to squeezed margins across an industry and competitive pressures that are higher than ever.

Secondly, the competitors you are benchmarking against may not be the ones that customers deem to be viable alternatives. Anchoring prices on irrelevant benchmarks instead of a deep understanding of the value created for customers can stifle growth and profitability.

Why you should not be overly led by the competition

Deciding your prices based solely on competitor prices cedes control of your pricing strategy to others and may misalign your pricing with what customers actually value about your product or service.

One sustainability startup launching a new platform to help organizations track their carbon footprint worked with us to validate their pricing strategy. For their customers, this would be a large enterprise purchase.

The team's pricing decisions were largely based on other emerging players in the market. But during customer interviews, we uncovered a surprising truth: their customers weren't even aware of the other players in the market, much less what their prices would be.

In fact, the market was so nascent that during an interview one customer casually compared the software to Netflix (despite the fact that Netflix is roughly 200 times cheaper than the price of the advanced software they had been introduced to).

This revealing moment highlighted the need for a shift. The team realized their reliance on competitor benchmarks was misplaced because their customers weren't looking at competitors at all. Instead, they turned their attention to educating customers about the unique value and outcomes of their product. They set their own pricing anchors, built a strong value narrative, and dropped the obsession with competitor prices that no one else seemed to care about.

By rethinking their strategy, they moved away from the constraints of competitor-led pricing and towards a more outcome-led approach, positioning their product on the basis of its value rather than irrelevant price comparisons.

Leverage Internal Data

Every organization, whether a startup or an established enterprise, has a treasure trove of internal data that when properly analysed can reveal the pathways to greater growth and profitability. By diving into this data, you can identify which activities, products or services are driving profits and which are draining resources. With this knowledge in hand, you can strategically adjust your focus to amplify the high-profit areas and re-evaluate or reimagine those that underperform.

For example, by looking at the juxtaposition of margin and growth, you can see which areas of your business are expanding profitably and which are stagnating or declining. For many companies, the high-growth areas present the most promising opportunities for refining or expanding pricing strategies to drive for profitability. However, maximizing profit isn't the sole objective for every organization. For mission-driven organizations, understanding areas of profit and growth enables you to strike the right balance by strategically using high-profitability areas to help fund low-profit, high-purpose parts of the business.

Leveraging internal data provides critical insights that can guide your team to:

1. Pinpoint where efforts should be concentrated, enabling your team to work smarter, not harder, by prioritizing the most impactful areas of the business.

2. Adapt your pricing strategy for different areas of the business, ensuring that you're responsive to changing market demand and internal performance.

3. Use the insights gained to inform broader business decisions, from resource allocation and hiring to investment and sales strategies.

We recommend creating a Growth-Profitability Matrix to visualize where the existing pockets of high growth and profitability lie within a business. It's a tool that was originally inspired by Calandro and Lane,[1] and has evolved through years of working with clients to become a powerful visualization tool.

Get started by plotting or categorizing your products or services into one of the four quadrants on the Growth-Profitability Matrix. This can be an exercise grounded in hard data or a more anecdotal perspective based on your team's collective insights, depending on the availability and accuracy of your profitability data.

The y-axis reflects growth rate – for example, year-on-year revenue or volume growth. This indicates the growth trajectory of a particular area of the business and can be classified into high or low growth. The x-axis reflects the level of profitability – for example, gross margin. This can also be classified into high or low.

Figure 2.3 illustrates the Growth-Profitability Matrix and its four quadrants. Each quadrant highlights a different category of offerings and can help guide pricing and portfolio decisions. Depending on where a product or service sits, it may be a candidate for one of the following strategic directions:

- **Star (high growth / high profitability).** Consider scaling
- **Favourite (high growth / low profitability).** Consider simplifying or repricing
- **Forgotten (low growth / low profitability).** Consider divesting
- **Puzzle (low growth / high profitability).** Consider reframing or cross-selling

Once you become comfortable with analysing your growth and profitability data through this lens, you can plot different cuts of the data to reveal broader insights. For service-based businesses, this method can be extended to compare growth and profitability between different customer segments or subscription tiers. Product-based businesses can apply the same principles by plotting growth and profitability across product ranges, categories, distribution channels, customer segments or geographical areas.

To divide the matrix into quadrants, you'll need to determine what counts as 'high' or 'low' growth and profitability. These thresholds can be based on absolute targets (e.g. 10% growth, 50% margin) or relative to your own data set

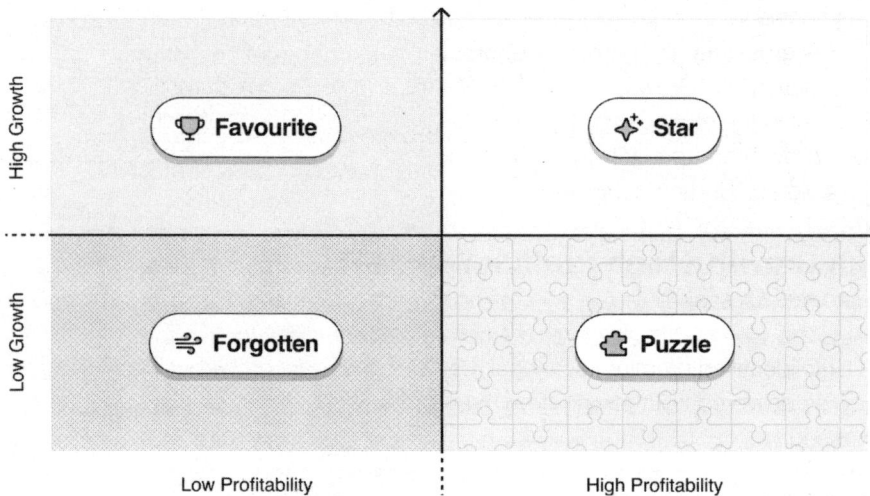

Figure 2.3 Growth-Profitability Matrix.

(e.g. above or below the median). Use thresholds that make strategic sense for your business and that help you distinguish between standout performers and underperformers. This approach reveals new insights into what is driving growth and what might be holding it back across different parts of your business.

Let's see how Pour & Prosper Coffee Co. has used the Growth-Profitability Matrix to reveal some unexpected trends in the business. In Figure 2.4, each bubble represents a product category. The size of each bubble represents the total revenue from the category in the last 12 months. Its position on the vertical

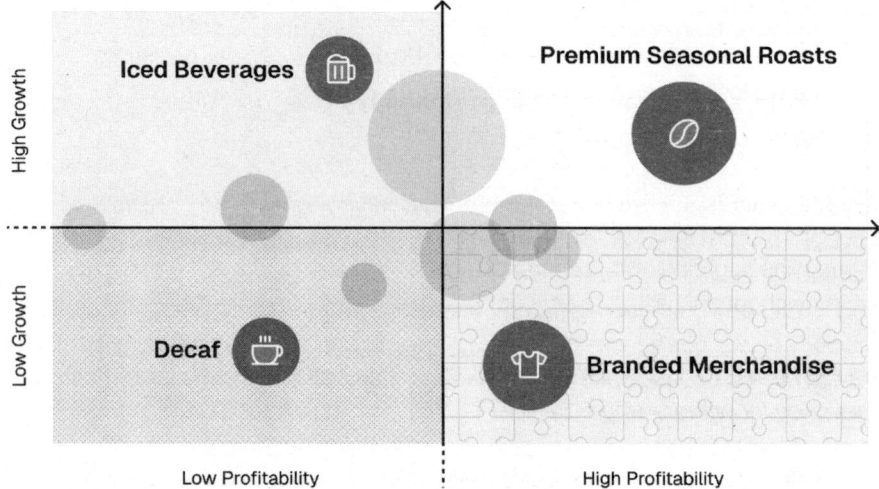

Figure 2.4 Growth-Profitability Matrix for Pour & Prosper Coffee Co.

y-axis shows year-on-year sales volume growth, while its position on the x-axis indicates gross margin for that category.

Populating the Growth-Profitability Matrix revealed some surprising insights and enabled the management team to have critical conversations about what is driving growth and profitability in the business. Here are some of the questions they explored for each quadrant:

High Growth / High Profitability – Stars
Candidates for scaling

The CFO identified premium seasonal roasts as the Stars of the business. These products delivered both strong growth and the highest margins. Here, the team discussed:

- What can we learn from here and cascade elsewhere?
- How might we accelerate growth in this category?

The result: the success of seasonal roasts was attributed to their limited-time availability and high perceived value among customers. The team decided to scale up visibility of these products during the festive season and explore year-round variations to build on this momentum without eroding the brand's premium perception.

High Growth / Low Profitability – Favourites
Candidates for simplification or repricing

Iced beverages emerged as Favourites, driving considerable growth but delivering lower-than-average margins. This led the team to ask:

- Are we losing margin unnecessarily?
- Are we comfortable with forgoing margin here?

A deeper analysis revealed that higher ingredient costs and preparation time were reducing profitability. The team decided to work with the operations team to streamline sourcing and preparation processes, leading to an improvement in margins without sacrificing quality or customer satisfaction.

Low Growth / Low Profitability – Forgottens
Candidates for withdrawing from offering

Decaf coffee was plotted in the low growth, low margin quadrant – the Forgotten category. Two key questions were on the team's mind:

- Are we seeing non-monetary benefits?
- Are there external factors restricting performance?

Decaf coffee had slow growth due to its niche appeal and lower profitability driven by higher bean costs. While it contributed minimally to margin and growth, the team recognized its importance in maintaining a 'complete' coffee shop offering and appealing to those who need or prefer decaf. Rather than discontinuing it or pricing it higher than caffeinated options, the team sourced more cost-effective decaf beans to maintain quality and price parity while improving profitability.

Low Growth / High Profitability – Puzzle
Candidates for reframing or cross-selling

The branded merchandise line, including mugs and thermoses, fell into the Puzzle quadrant. These products delivered high margins but had relatively low growth. This made the team wonder:

- What might be limiting our traction in this area?
- Do we want to invest in growth here?

To increase traction, the team proposed bundling merchandise with seasonal roasts or gift card promotions, turning them into attractive add-ons for customers and boosting overall revenue.

After completing the matrix, the team were surprised by how many levers there were for improving revenue or profitability without even changing the price. So much so, the team constructed a second Growth-Profitability Matrix, this time comparing the relative performance of each store (rather than product categories). The matrix revealed differing profitability and growth patterns between urban and suburban stores, prompting targeted campaigns and tailored pricing strategies for each location. This iterative use of the matrix became an invaluable tool for ensuring the business continued to grow sustainably and profitably.

Examine Customer Behaviours

To complement your new understanding of where growth and profitability sit in the business, examining existing customer behaviours can surface additional clues and insights into how your customers engage with your current pricing and options.

Analysis	Look for
Purchase trends	Which products or services are most popular? How does this differ by customer profile?
Repeat purchase and upsell behaviours	Which add-ons or additional services are most popular? Which customers are most likely to want more?
Lifetime value drivers	What behaviours drive retention and lifetime value? Which customers are most likely to churn?
Response to prior price changes or experiments	What did you learn from historic price changes or experiments that involved price? How did customer behaviours and conversion rates change?
Effectiveness of discounting	What has been the response to discounts or price promotions? How does this change by depth or type of discount offered?
Product popularity	Which product variants are most popular? Which are the most complementary product categories for cross-selling?
Feature or offering engagement	Which elements of your offering are most used or valued? Are customers making full use of what they've purchased? Are they upgrading, expanding or deepening their relationship with you over time?

Figure 2.5 Customer behaviours.

The list of behaviours and patterns in Figure 2.5 offers a useful starting point for investigation. While data-rich businesses may conduct more detailed analysis, these suggestions can provide valuable inspiration for any organization.

In this chapter, you set out to understand what truly drives or limits profitability within your organization. Like a fishing expedition, you might have landed on a gold mine of pricing insights or may have walked away with just one or two big 'ahas!' to point you in the right direction. To illustrate how uncovering insights from existing data can help teams move from discovery to actionable opportunities to test later in the Pricing Sprint process, let's explore a few illustrative scenarios:

- **A technology company** discovered 80% of its customers subscribed to their highest tier, while only 5% opted for the entry-level option. This insight signalled an opportunity to introduce a new, higher-priced tier that could cater to those customers willing to pay more for additional value.

- **A retail business** observed that customers only responded to promotions offering over 20% off. This insight suggested the need to refine the promotional calendar to focus on fewer deeper discounts that resonate with customer expectations and drive sales.

- **A subscription business** realized only a minority of its customers use certain built-in features. These features were repositioned as add-ons, allowing the business to tailor its offerings and charge accordingly based on what customers truly value.

- **A professional services firm** found that its deal conversion rate was significantly higher in the retail sector than in the travel industry. This insight prompted the team to refine their value messaging and shift to higher prices for retailers while reconsidering their approach for the less responsive travel operators.

In each of these scenarios, the insights gleaned from internal data, customer sentiment analysis and competitor pricing were like catching that big fish – a moment of clarity that transformed the team's approach. These discoveries went on to guide the focus of each team's Pricing Sprint in different ways, from designing new product tiers to adjusting promotional strategies, bundling/ unbundling features to refining their market focus.

Set the Parameters for Your Pricing Sprint

You likely began this chapter with an idea of what you wanted to focus on in your Pricing Sprint. Like in the scenarios you just read, sometimes the biggest opportunities surface in unexpected places and what you thought you'd tackle might no longer be the most important thing to achieve.

Now's the time to take stock. Revisit the decisions you captured in your Pricing Strategy Blueprint back in Chapter 1. What did you commit to maintain, pivot or explore? Then, look at what surfaced in this chapter as you uncovered hidden opportunities. Do your original priorities still hold? Or is it time to adjust course based on what you know now?

This next step will help you set clear parameters for the sprint ahead so you're focused, aligned and working on the things that matter most. You'll explore two key questions with your Sprint team:

- What do we change?
- How big of a change are we ready for?

Start by considering which of the following elements of pricing the team is willing and interested in exploring as you continue your Pricing Sprint. Using Pricing

Sprint Parameters listed in Figure 2.6, ask the team to indicate their relative tolerance for change within each parameter using the following scale:

1 – Strong preference to maintain. Change is unnecessary or harmful.

2 – Mild preference to maintain. The status quo is mostly working.

3 – Neutral / open. Open to change if it adds clear value.

4 – Mild preference to change. Ready for thoughtful change.

5 – Strong preference to change. We should actively pursue change now.

After the team has given each parameter a score, collate the results and start to prioritize where you want to go next based on the areas of interest for the team and time you've allocated for your first sprint. This helps align ambition with reality, keeps the focus on what matters most and avoids time spent on topics that are already off the table.

Pricing Sprint Parameters	Score
Value messaging: Should we change how we talk about our pricing? *For example, enhancing product or service descriptions, highlighting customer outcomes or incorporating customer testimonials?*	
Product or service configuration: Should we change how we package our existing offer? *For example, creating bundles, introducing upsells or repackaging offerings*	
Pricing presentation: Should we change how pricing is visually presented? *For example, pricing pages, proposals or checkout screens.*	
Pricing model: Should we change how we charge? *For example, moving from a per-unit model to usage-based pricing or moving from hourly rates to project-based fees.*	
Price points: Should we change how much we charge? *For example, raising or lowering prices or setting different prices for different users.*	
Pricing strategy: Should we change our commercial strategy? *For example, targeting different segments, business goals or market positioning.*	
Promotional mechanisms: Should we change promotions and discounts? *For example, reducing discounting or adding limited-time offers, referral incentives, seasonal discounts or bundle promotions?*	

Figure 2.6 Pricing Sprint parameters.

For example, if you started out anticipating running **a short and focused sprint** and you find that your team's interest is limited to cosmetic pricing such as value messaging and price presentation, you know you are on the right track. However, if there's a strong appetite for change across all or most of the sprint parameters, then now is the time to shift to a **longer, more exploratory sprint**.

Plan Your Next Step

The insights you've uncovered in this chapter have helped your team zero in on the areas of pricing with the greatest opportunity and appetite for change. Keep these findings close. Your team will revisit them in the chapters ahead as you begin connecting the dots between business data, customer insight and market realities.

In the next chapter, you'll start the design phase of your sprint. This is a creative stretch of the sprint where your team begins to shape how pricing might work differently in the future. You'll create a customer-facing prototype that brings your ideas to life in a way your team and customers can see, experience and respond to.

PRICING PLAYBOOK: UNCOVER HIDDEN OPPORTUNITIES

Take these six steps to identify where to focus your efforts first:

1. **Map your pricing process**
   Capture how pricing decisions are made today, who's involved and where bottlenecks appear.

2. **Explore customer sentiment**
   Review testimonials, support tickets, reviews and feedback to surface clues about how customers respond to your pricing today.

3. **Benchmark the competition**
   Track competitor pricing to understand how others position their offer and where you sit in the market.

4. **Leverage internal data**
   Dig into your data to identify which customers, products or services are most (and least) profitable.

5. **Examine customer behaviours**

Spot trends in buying patterns, upgrade paths and churn. Use these clues to uncover pricing friction and potential growth levers.

6. **Set the parameters for your Pricing Sprint**

Gauge your team's appetite for change and use it to shape the focus and scale of your sprint.

Design

3
MAKE IDEAS TANGIBLE

Before your marketing team launches a new campaign, they don't just talk about it, they make it real. They write draft copy, test headlines, create mock-ups or run small experiments to see what lands. These early versions aren't perfect, and they're not meant to be. They exist to spark ideas, invite feedback and make improvements before a big launch.

Yet when it comes to rethinking pricing, the process is often far less deliberate. Teams often rely on gut instinct or make changes behind closed doors only to wait and see how customers react once it's live. It may feel like the only option (after all, what customer is going to tell you they want to pay more?), but this approach often leads to pricing decisions that don't land with customers and can't easily be undone.

Without a way to put a pricing change in front of customers early, it can feel impossible to get real input before a decision has to be made. You need something that is real enough to react to, flexible enough to change before launch, and safe enough to avoid triggering unnecessary pushback from your customers. That's where prototyping comes in.

A Pricing Prototype is a simple, visual draft of your pricing ideas. It's intentionally low-fidelity – think a basic mock-up on a single slide or page. It's designed to invite feedback, first from your internal team, then from customers.

The process of creating a prototype together creates two powerful shifts in how your sprint team makes decisions: it moves from debating to doing and from opinion-based disagreement to evidence-led testing. Let's take each one in turn.

Let's start with the mindset of 'doing over debating'. Instead of endlessly debating what you *should do*, you first explore what you *could do*. Without committing too soon, you can visualize how the customer would see alternative pricing models, different product bundles, or new ways of presenting your offer. A quick sketch of a pricing page, a mocked-up proposal or a new offer laid out in a slide is often all it takes to spark the right conversations and move your thinking forward.

Once your sprint team is aligned on the possible directions, it's time to shift gears. You adopt the mindset of 'we don't fight, we test'. This means bringing your leading prototype(s) into the field to see how it lands with the people it's really for – your customers – and letting the evidence lead you to the best solution. By testing in a low-risk, controlled way, it reduces the chances of a pricing change backfiring and increases your odds of landing on something that delivers real results.

In this chapter, you'll learn how to bring your pricing ideas to life through simple prototypes that spark valuable conversations both internally and externally. Even if the thought of sharing your ideas before they're finalized feels uncomfortable at first, you'll quickly see how prototypes can reduce risk and help your team move forward with greater clarity and confidence.

Identify What to Prototype

Your first stop is deciding what to prototype. When customers interact with your brand and first see your pricing, they form an impression that influences their decision to buy. This is the moment of truth: the point in the journey where they form an opinion about your pricing, and decide whether to move forward or walk away. That's the moment you want to prototype.

For a software subscription, this could mean mocking up changes to the pricing page on your website. For enterprise-level services, it might mean reimagining the pricing section of a proposal document. In e-commerce, it could be a combination of product pages and checkout screens that guide the user through their purchase journey.

To find your pricing moment of truth, return to the parameters you set at the end of Chapter 2. These parameters capture what aspects of your pricing are open for change during your Pricing Sprint, whether it's how your pricing is presented, structured or set. Use them to guide your focus for prototyping. Start with the area that has the greatest potential to influence what your customer sees or experiences before they buy. Figure 3.1 maps common prototype ideas to each parameter. It's not exhaustive, but it should give you a solid starting point to get ideas flowing.

Once you identify what your moment of truth might be, capture a snapshot of what that moment looks like today – literally. Save the file, take a screenshot or print it out. If you already have ideas for what needs to change, mark it up, highlight, scribble, comment, whatever helps capture your early thinking. If you're not sure what to change yet, that's fine too. Read on, and you'll shape your prototype as you go.

Parameter	The Change	Prototype Idea
Value messaging	How we talk about price	A revised landing page highlighting value through outcomes or testimonials
Product or service configuration	How we package our offer	The pricing page of your website or proposal showing a 'good-better-best' tiered offer
Pricing presentation	How pricing is visually presented	The pricing page of your website or proposal applying nudges from Chapter 4
Pricing model	How we charge	The pricing page of your website or proposal mocked up as it would be with the new model
Price points	How much we charge	A mock-up of the offer with the new price
Pricing strategy	How pricing impacts strategy	Choose a format from one of the other parameters that shows how your strategy shift would be experienced by the customer
Promotional mechanisms	How we use promotions and discounts	A mock-up of a limited-time offer page or a referral programme concept slide

Figure 3.1 Prototype ideas based on parameter.

Embrace the Power of Prototyping

'Building prototypes made the future model really tangible. They helped to set the vision for where we wanted to go and ultimately allowed us to all start rowing in the same direction.'

KARIM MORGAN NEHDI *Founder & CEO of Herrmann HBDI®*

Designing a Pricing Prototype is about the journey as much as it is the destination. Most likely, the first prototype you design is not the same as the one you will launch with. Prototyping is a process of exploration and discovery that allows your team to test, iterate and refine.

Even before a prototype is tested with customers, there is immense value in the process of designing and iterating it within your team. It allows you to:

- **Build buy-in.** Prototyping collaboratively invites your team to explore various pricing concepts, engage in the creative process, and contribute ideas that might not have surfaced otherwise. This collaboration not only strengthens the pricing strategy but also ensures that the entire team is aligned and invested in the final approach.

- **Explore different models.** Iterating on multiple solutions increases the likelihood of success. A study by IDEO* found that product launches are 50% more likely to succeed when teams explore five or more different solutions. The same principle extends to the launch of a new pricing model or planning price changes. Applying an exploratory approach allows you to weigh the benefits and drawbacks of each approach, helping you zero in on the most viable options.

- **Assess risk tolerance.** Innovations in pricing, like product development, can range from incremental to radical. Creating a range of prototypes lets you gauge your Pricing Sprint team's risk tolerance and determine which pricing strategies align best with your overall objectives. Is the team prepared to make only minor cosmetic changes to the way that the price is presented or are they looking to tear up the underlying pricing model and start again (or somewhere in between)?

The real magic then happens when you test your prototype with customers. This testing phase can take various forms, depending on your needs and starting point. You might test changes in a customer interview (see Chapter 5), validate an entirely new model at scale in a quantitative survey (see Chapter 6), run live A/B tests (see Chapter 7), or use a combination of methods to iteratively design, then test to gather evidence that validates (or not!) different ideas.

Regardless of the method, testing your prototype with customers allows you to:

- **Gauge reactions and mitigate risks.** Introducing new pricing ideas to a controlled group of customers to gather feedback and make adjustments before a full-scale launch, reducing the risk of market rejection and costly mistakes.

- **Enhance customer understanding.** Along the way, you'll collect a range of perceptions about value and what unlocks willingness to pay. This direct feedback helps you refine your pricing strategy, ensuring that it resonates with your target audience and aligns with the perceived value of your offerings.

---

*IDEO's research, based on 26 years of client projects and external sources, identified experimentation as one of six qualities shared by adaptable, innovative organizations.[1]

- **Identify optimal price points.** A tangible prototype enables more accurate testing of willingness to pay as it simulates the moment when customers experience your pricing.

Why you should prototype (even if you think you've got it figured out)

Prototyping offers a powerful way to align on vision, surface critical questions and uncover new perspectives.

Herrmann, the creators of HBDI® assessment tool, used a Pricing Sprint to reimagine their pricing model. Here's how two of the team described the impact of using prototypes during their journey:

"Prototyping the pricing model surfaced a lot of those tricky questions that we have talked about and kept brushing aside. It brought them to a head, along with some of the practical and technical implications of moving to a new model."

-Virlina Choquette, Chief of Staff

"I came into this with a set mind of what a pricing model should look like from what I've known and where I was in the past. However, we learned that a pricing model could look quite different across the board from looking at many different other companies and how they do it. There's a different shape for every company."

-Wendy Schoeman, Head of Client Success

Gather Inspiration

With your Prototyping Parameters clearly defined, the next step is to draw inspiration from the market. This isn't about copying others but identifying ideas that might resonate with your audience. Gathering inspiration can catalyse creativity and spark new ideas, especially when it comes from a range of sources, from direct competitors to innovators in completely different markets.

A powerful tool to achieve this is Lightning Demos, which were originally introduced as part of Google's Design Sprint[2] methodology. The idea behind a Lightning Demo is to quickly gather, share and analyse examples of inspiring pricing tactics. This process enables your team to see how others have solved similar challenges, sparking new ideas that can be adapted and refined to suit your specific needs.

To run a Lightning Demo session, ask each team member to seek out examples of pricing they've seen 'in the wild' that stand out to them. Examples may be from within your industry and beyond; ideally, across the team you will have a balance of both. Have each team member pick one to three of their most powerful examples and create a quick visual card that can be shared with the team, which includes:

- **A screenshot.** The visual moment of truth where the customer sees the pricing.
- **Things you like.** In three simple bullets, answer 'What I like about this is . . .'
- **Ideas this sparks.** In one to three simple bullets, answer 'What if we . . .'

Encourage everyone to keep their cards clear and concise – think headlines, not essays! Collect the cards in a shared space, or better yet, hold a collaboration session where each team member spends 2 minutes presenting their examples.

This activity will serve as seeds for innovative pricing ideas. Once everyone has shared their Lightning Demo, spend time evaluating these statements, prioritizing them based on anticipated effort and impact. This process will help you focus on the high-priority ideas you want to test, ensuring that your approach is both inventive and grounded in practical realities.

Amazon often makes an appearance in Lightning Demos we run with clients. As you will see in Figure 3.2, its pricing pages are rich with tactics that influence customer behaviour, such as free returns to reduce perceived risk, subscription discounts to nudge recurring revenue, and delivery incentives to increase average order value. Even for businesses outside retail or e-commerce, examples like this help teams recognize transferable ideas and spark practical 'What if we . . .' thinking. Looking outside to see what others are doing allows you to draw on new inspiration and kick-start your prototyping process.

Create a Prototype (or Five)

By now, you've identified your pricing moment of truth and gathered inspiration and ideas for how pricing might work differently in the future. The next step is to bring those ideas to life by sketching out your first Pricing Prototype.

Prototyping can be a fast, inclusive exercise that brings the right people and ideas together without consuming endless hours. You might choose to have one team member create a few options, or ask each member to develop their own. The best approach depends on your team's size and level of alignment. For

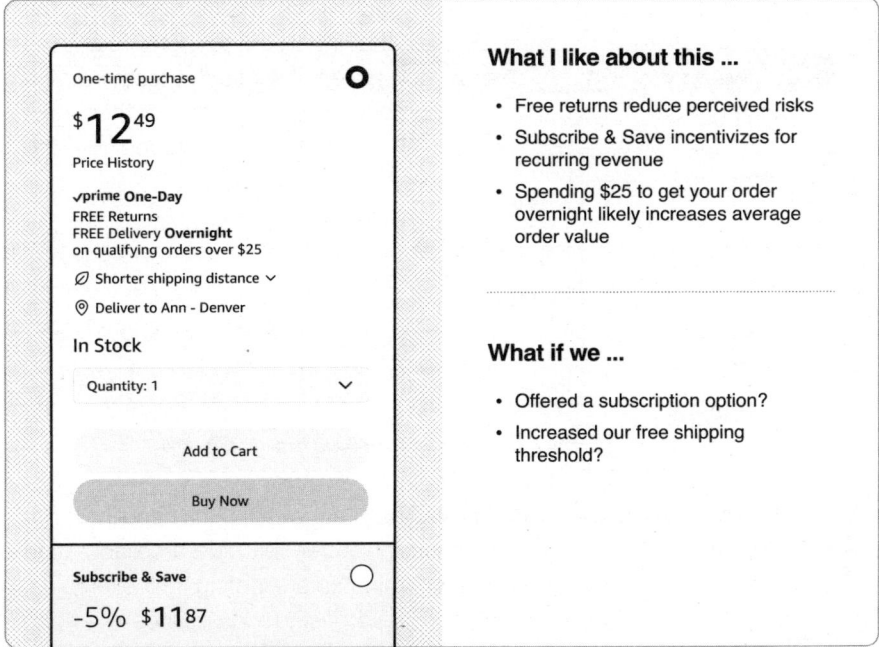

One-time purchase   ⬤

$**12**⁴⁹

Price History

✓prime **One-Day**
FREE Returns
FREE Delivery **Overnight**
on qualifying orders over $25

⬗ Shorter shipping distance ⌄

◉ Deliver to Ann - Denver

In Stock

Quantity: 1   ⌄

Add to Cart

Buy Now

Subscribe & Save   ◯

-5% $**11**⁸⁷

What I like about this ...

- Free returns reduce perceived risks
- Subscribe & Save incentivizes for recurring revenue
- Spending $25 to get your order overnight likely increases average order value

What if we ...

- Offered a subscription option?
- Increased our free shipping threshold?

Figure 3.2 Example of an Amazon Lightning Demo.

smaller or closely aligned teams, nominating a single prototype owner can speed things up. For larger teams or those with diverse perspectives, inviting multiple people to sketch their ideas can help surface different viewpoints.

What you create doesn't need to be polished or perfect. In fact, starting with a low-fidelity prototype that is easy to change and adapt can be more beneficial. When your prototype looks unfinished and open to influence, you invite more open, honest feedback. The goal at this stage is to welcome feedback and encourage iteration. That's why early in the process, it can be effective to build a simple wireframe or mock-up using accessible tools like PowerPoint and Miro, or even a classic pencil and paper.

Start with the visual you already identified, your pricing moment of truth. That's what you'll turn into a working prototype. If needed, rebuild it into a simple format the whole team can access and interact with. To make sure your prototype is clear, structured and ready for feedback, check that it includes a few essential elements:

1. **Heading.** The one big thing that sets this option/offer apart. Help the reader grasp the concept from the outset.

2. **Value statement.** A punchy value proposition statement to signpost what differentiates one option from another.

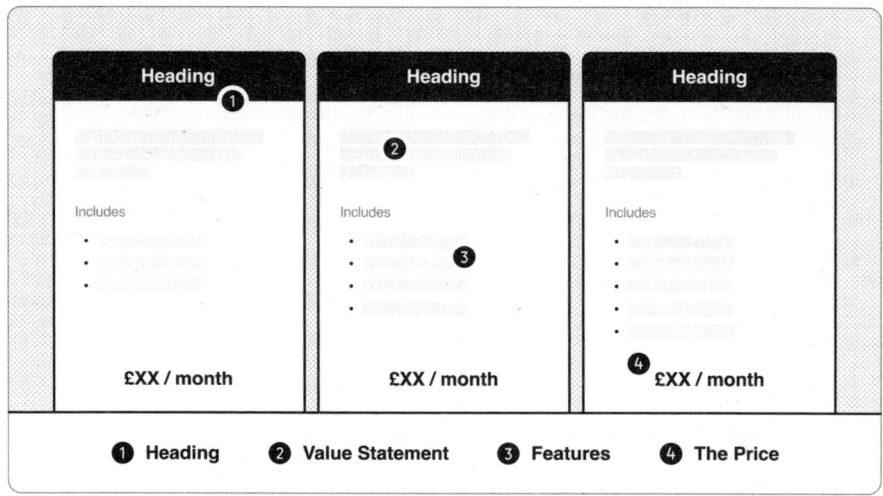

Figure 3.3 Prototype template for a tiered solution.

3. **Differentiation.** The features or components that are unique to each option or offering that make for an easy comparison.
4. **The price.** The cost for each option and how it's charged (one-time, monthly, annually).

Figure 3.3 illustrates how this might look for a typical tiered offering, such as a subscription or service offering. How each of these elements manifests visually may look very different depending on the ideas you want to test and if you are selling a bundled offering, a single product or something else entirely!

Follow these Prototyping Principles

Whether you're prototyping a subtle shift in how pricing is framed, exploring alternative promotional tactics or reimagining your pricing model entirely, remember your goal is to enable testing so you can learn what works before committing.

Over the years, we've helped teams prototype everything from minor tweaks to tiered structures through to major pricing model changes. Across that broad spectrum of experiences, three core principles have consistently emerged. They form a reliable foundation for designing pricing in ways that universally resonate with customers.

1. Offer choice

When preparing your prototype(s), keep in mind that offering choices at different price points is a powerful technique. Moving the customer from the binary decision 'Should I buy this?' to 'Which option should I choose?' can have a significant impact on their likelihood to buy.* Ensure that your prototype reflects this principle by offering clear, differentiated choices that are easy for customers to understand.

Common ways to differentiate your options:

- Adjust the features or deliverables that are included.
- Change the level of service or support.
- Adjust usage limits, delivery speed or access duration.
- Vary commitment length or payment terms.

Offering choices also allows you to:

- Create an upsell path.
- Strengthen your position in negotiations by clearly linking price to scope.
- Tap into a wider range of customer needs and budgets.
- Anchor price perception more effectively.

2. Price the cake, not the ingredients

Focusing on the overall value that your customers will receive, rather than the individual components that make up the product or service, helps position your offering as a complete solution and makes the purchase decision feel easier and more compelling.

- **Present a package.** Rather than breaking down individual services or features with separate costs, offer a single price that bundles together all of the components. Shift feature lists and specifications to be lower in the hierarchy so that customers can still access the details they need when they need them.

---

*The book *Predictably Irrational* illustrates how introducing a third option can produce a 'decoy effect' that steers customer choice.[3]

- **Focus on the outcome.** Clearly articulate the overarching benefits, results or outcomes, emphasizing how the whole is greater than the sum of its parts. Bring to life how individual services or features come together to create a solution that meets your customers' needs.

- **Use customer language.** Ensure that the way you describe the value aligns with how your customers think and talk about their needs and challenges. Avoid technical jargon and instead use terms that resonate with your audience's day-to-day experiences.

By pricing the 'cake' as a complete, value-driven solution, you position the purchase decision in a way that is both more meaningful and more persuasive to customers. In some cases, such as public sector proposals, customers may prefer or even insist on detailed price breakdowns. In these situations, try to maintain the focus on overall value and investment, even if you still have to include the detailed breakdowns.

3. Reduce the cognitive load

The easier it is for customers to make a decision, the more likely they are to proceed with a purchase. Cognitive overload, where a customer is bombarded with too much information or too many choices, can cause decision fatigue and lead to hesitation or abandonment. To counteract this, your prototype should simplify the decision-making process as much as possible.

- **Present simple options.** Ensure that your options are clearly differentiated and signposted. Too many choices can overwhelm customers, so limit the options to those that cater to distinct needs or segments.

- **Consolidate information.** Ensure that all essential information is presented in a way that is easy to digest. Use clear headings, bullet points and concise language to reduce the mental effort required to understand the offerings.

- **Apply a visual hierarchy.** Structure your pricing page or proposal so that the most critical information stands out. Use visual cues such as size, colour and positioning to guide the customer's eye to the most important details.

By focusing on these principles, you'll be able to craft a Pricing Prototype that not only resonates with your customers but also guides them towards making confident, informed purchasing decisions.

Plan Your Next Step

With your Pricing Prototype in progress, your Pricing Sprint is now well underway. You've identified the key moment of truth where customers engage with your pricing, aligned your team around a shared vision for testing and refinement, and crafted initial prototypes that reflect potential changes to your pricing. These steps have introduced the next layer of clarity and intentional design to your pricing strategy.

In Chapter 4, we'll explore how small, subtle adjustments in the way pricing is presented to customers can profoundly influence customer behaviour. By leveraging behavioural nudges and psychological principles, you'll learn how to refine your prototype into a tool that not only resonates with your audience but also guides them towards confident purchasing decisions.

PRICING PLAYBOOK: MAKE IDEAS TANGIBLE

Take these five steps to bring your ideas to life:

1. **Identify what to prototype**
   Identify the pricing moment of truth where customers first see or interact with your pricing.

2. **Set prototyping parameters**
   Gauge your team's appetite for change across pricing model, structure and messaging. Agree what's on the table to change.

3. **Gather inspiration**
   Collect bold ideas and tactics from other brands, industries and competitors to fuel your thinking.

4. **Create your prototype**
   Turn ideas into something clear and tangible that you can share with others, iterate as a team and prepare for customer testing.

5. **Refine with proven prototyping principles**
   Use proven techniques to offer clear choices, emphasize overall value and reduce cognitive load for your customer.

4

NUDGE BEHAVIOURS

Now for a little bit of magic.

We're going to show you how to tap into the way people think and decide, using cognitive biases to your advantage in ways that are ethical, effective and deeply human. And the best part? You don't need to change the actual price, just how you present it.

How you present pricing sends powerful signals that shape how customers perceive value, compare options and, ultimately, decide what to buy. Even the smallest changes, or *nudges*, can dramatically improve how prices are understood.

These subtle changes can outperform full-scale pricing overhauls, delivering real gains with far less risk. For one global brand, we introduced a series of subtle but strategic changes to how pricing was laid out on their website. The result? A 23% increase in average spend per session from new customers – without changing a single price point or discount. Just sharper, more psychologically attuned communication, using the very nudges you're about to see.

In this chapter, we're opening up our playbook and sharing ten of our most trusted pricing psychology nudges. These are science-backed techniques we use with clients across industries to influence decision-making, shift perception and make pricing feel easier to say yes to.

This part of the Pricing Sprint consistently delights our clients and the global audiences we speak with because once you see these nudges in action, you can't unsee them. You'll start to notice them everywhere: in stores, restaurant menus, subscription plans and checkout pages. And as you do, you'll start to spot opportunities in your own business. Are the numbers in large or small fonts? Are they rounded or precise? Are there choices, or just one offer?

If you've jumped straight to this chapter, these nudges can sharpen how you present your pricing today. If you're following the full Pricing Sprint and have already built a Pricing Prototype, this is your moment to infuse it with a little persuasive firepower. By incorporating these small nudges now, you'll fine-tune your prototype to resonate more deeply with your customers and ensure that it not only attracts attention, but influences behaviour in the right direction.

Let's dive into the first nudge and show you just how much a tiny nudge can do.

Nudge 1: Use Small Fonts for Price Points

Let's start with a straightforward yet highly effective nudge. Research shows that displaying prices in smaller font sizes can make them feel like smaller numbers. This effect is due to a cognitive bias where our brains link visual size with numerical size. When you present a price in a smaller font, customers are likely to perceive it as being less expensive.[1] This subtle change can influence purchasing decisions without altering the actual price, making it a powerful tool in your nudge toolkit.

Nudge 2: Shorten the Visual Length of Your Prices

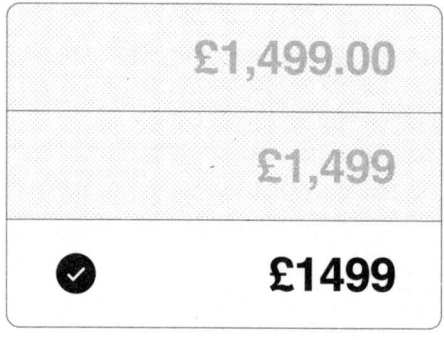

This nudge shows that how you format your price can make it seem lower to customers. Research published in the *Journal of Consumer Psychology* found that the way prices are written, particularly the use of commas and decimal points, impacts how customers perceive the cost.[2] To simplify the findings, imagine you could show three variations of the same price:

1. £1,499.00 (with comma and pence)
2. £1,499 (without pence)
3. £1499 (without comma and pence)

Although the numerical value is identical, the third price, written without any commas or decimals, feels the lowest. This occurs because the addition of symbols and numbers increases the brain's processing time, and numbers that require a longer time to process are perceived as being larger. In contrast, prices with shorter visual length are quicker and simpler to process, which subconsciously makes them feel like a lower cost.

Watch for this nudge as you go about your day. It's common to see coffee shops and high-end restaurants omitting the comma, pence and even the currency symbol to keep prices super simple. So, when presenting your own prices, scrap unnecessary decimal places, drop the commas and keep your prices simple.

Nudge 3: Use Charm Pricing

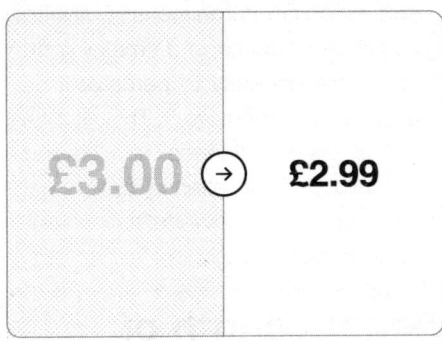

Sometimes, shaving just one penny off a price can have a surprisingly large impact. That's the logic behind charm pricing, a widely used technique where prices ending in .99 (or .95) feel significantly lower than their rounded counterparts. The impact is most significant when the leftmost digit decreases. For instance, changing a price from £2.80 to £2.79 won't make much difference. But reducing a price from £3.00 to £2.99 doesn't just save one penny, it makes the price feel disproportionately lower.[3] Why? Because in Western cultures, numbers are read from left to right. The first digit someone sees becomes an anchor, shaping their perception of the magnitude of the entire price before they've even finished reading it. This means that a one-penny reduction can feel like a one-pound difference to your customer.

That said, charm pricing isn't always the best fit. Research shows that non-rounded prices (such as £39.99) are more effective when customers are making logical, deliberate decisions such as purchasing office supplies. By contrast, rounded prices (such as £200) are better suited to emotionally driven purchases such as buying a designer watch.[4]

Nudge 4: Add Social Proof

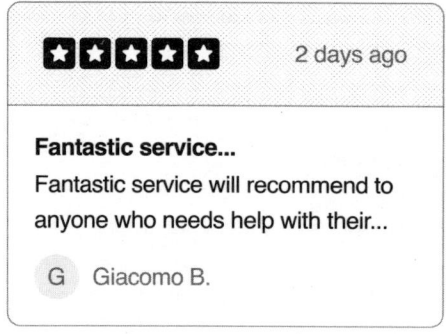

When customers see that others have made the same choice, they're more likely to follow suit. That's why simple phrases like 'Most Popular' or 'Bestseller' can dramatically influence purchase decisions.[5] These cues reduce decision fatigue and create a sense of reassurance by tapping into our natural tendency to conform.

You can amplify this effect by embedding social proof directly alongside your pricing information. Customer logos, short testimonials and star ratings placed near your pricing create immediate trust signals. The impact is even greater when that proof is verifiable. If you're using platforms like Google Reviews or Trustpilot, include links or visuals that confirm authenticity. Including these small cues right alongside your pricing builds confidence and subtly reassures customers that choosing you is both popular and low risk.

Nudge 5: Anchor with Any High Number

People rarely evaluate prices in a vacuum. Instead, they compare them, often unconsciously, to other numbers they have just seen. This is the anchoring effect, a powerful cognitive bias where an initial number sets a reference point and influences how subsequent values are perceived.

That anchor does not need to be directly related to price. Simply placing a high number near your pricing, such as 'Join 20,000 happy users' or 'Was £199, now £129', can make your actual price seem more reasonable. In a well-known experiment by MIT's Dan Ariely,[6] participants were asked to write down the last two digits of their Social Security Number before bidding on various items. Those with higher numbers were willing to pay significantly more, sometimes up to three times as much, despite the digits having no real connection to the products.

In your own pricing, you can apply this effect in subtle but powerful ways. Showing a pre-discounted price, referencing a large user base or highlighting a high-value donation total are all forms of anchoring. Even just positioning a premium tier first in your pricing layout (as we explore in Nudge 8) can help establish a higher anchor point. These cues reframe how the actual price is judged and often make it feel more acceptable, even attractive, by comparison.

Nudge 6: Show Real People

Emotions often drive purchase decisions more than logic, and that is where the affect principle comes in. Showing images of real people alongside your pricing information taps into this emotional layer, helping customers feel more connected, reassured and confident in their choice.

This could be a photo of your team behind the scenes, a customer enjoying your product or a brand ambassador sharing their story. The key is relatability. When people see faces that reflect their own experiences, aspirations or values, it produces a 'people like me' effect, increasing relevance and trust.

Including real people next to pricing also humanizes the purchase. It makes the experience feel more personal and grounded rather than purely transactional. More importantly, it builds emotional credibility* by showing that your product is used and valued by people who matter to your prospective buyers. In the end, people don't buy products, they buy stories they see themselves in.

---

*One study in the *Quarterly Journal of Economics* found that adding a photo of a person smiling increased the demand for a loan by as much as a 25% drop in interest rate would have.[7]

Nudge 7: Reduce Choice

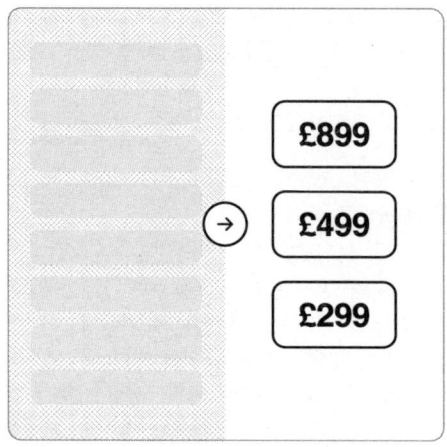

When customers face too much choice, they become overwhelmed. It's like standing in the cereal aisle, bombarded by options – high fibre, low sugar, great taste, gluten-free, heart-healthy, protein-packed. The more there are, the harder it is to choose.

Research across consumer goods and investments, retailers and manufacturers shows that when customers face an overwhelming number of options, they are more likely to defer, abandon or regret their decision.*

The nudge: Present enough variety to enable choice, but not so much that it overwhelms the buyer.

For product-based businesses, this means having an in-depth understanding of which products serve which jobs, where overlaps exist and how each one earns its place to ensure that each choice is well-targeted.

For service-based businesses, the same principle applies to the options you put forward to customers. Even when you think you know exactly what a customer needs, you can still present options, whether it's an upsell path that anticipates their future needs or a scaled-back version that creates room for negotiation. By curating the number of choices and making the differences between them meaningful, you reduce the noise, boost customer confidence and make it easier for them to say yes.

---

*One consumer goods study found that consumers were more likely to try jam at a tasting booth if they were presented with twenty-four flavours; however, they were more likely to actually purchase the sweet goodness when they only had six flavours to choose from.[8] A separate study of investments found that found that participation in 401(k) plans was higher when employees were presented with fewer than ten plans.[9] The work by Chernev et al. explored why more options lead to choice overload.[10]

Nudge 8: Sort Prices from High to Low

£119 £179 £249

£249 £179 £119

While it's common to see options laid out in increasing price order, like the familiar good-better-best or bronze-silver-gold structure, reversing this order can sometimes be more beneficial.

Starting with the highest price can trigger the anchoring effect.[11] When the most expensive option is listed first, it sets a high reference point, making the subsequent prices appear more reasonable and affordable by comparison. For those who value premium offerings, this initial high anchor could be the choice they gravitate towards. Even if they opt for a less expensive option, seeing the higher-priced option first anchors their perception of value, making the lower prices seem like better deals.

Anchoring is not the only psychological force at play. Loss aversion can also influence behaviour when prices are ordered from high to low. As customers progress through the options, each cheaper option may feel like a compromise. This perception can trigger a subtle sense of loss,[12] nudging customers towards a higher-priced option to avoid missing out on quality or value. Rather than feeling like they're saving money, they may feel as though they're giving something up.

Of course, there are times when the traditional method of ordering by increasing price has its place. A low-to-high price structure can be easier to understand when each tier progressively adds more features or value, or you are keen to convey a clear upsell path.

Nudge 9: Reframe the Price

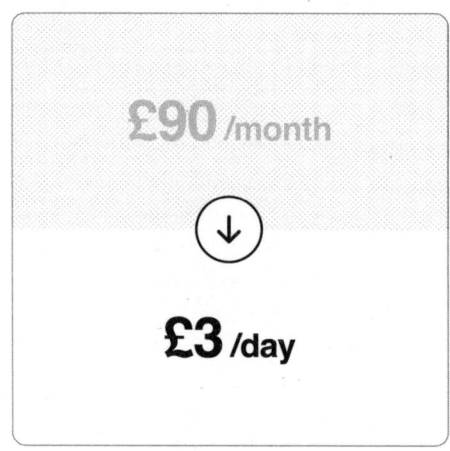

When customers evaluate a price, they interpret it through the lens of how they think about money. That's why framing your price in a way that aligns with their mental model can make it feel more manageable.

For example, for a consumer, a subscription fee of £90 per month may be easier to digest when framed as just £3 per day, comparable to the cost of a daily coffee. This breaks the cost into smaller, relatable chunks. The shift in perspective it creates can make the expense seem less significant and more easily justifiable.[13, 14]

The same principle can also work in reverse. For a business purchase, a buyer may think in terms of their annual budget. In this case, showing £36,000 per year instead of £3,000 per month removes the need for additional calculations. The price becomes instantly understandable in the context they use to make decisions.

The key is to present your price in a format that makes intuitive sense to your customer. When the frame of reference fits how they naturally think about cost, you remove unnecessary complexity and this makes it easier for them to say yes. How do you know what makes intuitive sense to your customer? You ask. Read more about testing prototypes and interviewing customers in Chapters 3 and 5.

Nudge 10: Tailor Discounts to Your Price Points

$130
$120
$110

$100

$ use absolute discounts

$90
$80
$70

% use percentage discounts

When offering discounts, the way you present them can significantly impact customer perception. For items priced below $100, customers perceive percentage discounts (like 20% off) as more valuable, while for items over $100, absolute discounts (such as $20 off) are seen as more appealing.[15]

This is because the numerical value appears larger and thus more compelling. For example, 20% off a $50 purchase is perceived as a better deal than $10 off, even though they are mathematically the same. Conversely, $30 off a $150 purchase feels like a better discount than 20% off, even though both offer the same savings.

Tailoring how you display your discounts in this way can enhance customer satisfaction and drive purchases by aligning with how people naturally evaluate value.

Put Nudges into Practice

"Nudges are like cheat codes for pricing: subtle, powerful and surprisingly effective at unlocking incremental margin."

EMMA KAMEL *Former UK General Manager, Naked Wines*

Incorporating these behavioural nudges into your pricing presentation is a powerful way to harness the science of decision-making to benefit both your customers and your business. By understanding the psychology behind how people perceive prices, you can create a more engaging and persuasive pricing experience that resonates with your target audience. These small yet impactful adjustments not only help to increase conversion but also enhance customer satisfaction by making purchasing decisions feel easier and more intuitive.

As you move forward, remember that the key to successful pricing isn't just the numbers but how those numbers are presented and framed. With the right nudges in your toolkit, you can transform your pricing information into a powerful asset to drive customer behaviours.*

---

*If you are ready for more practical psychological pricing nudges, we recommend checking out *The Psychology of Pricing*.[16]

To see how these nudges work in the real world, let's take a look at how Sprint Valley, a UK-based strategy consultancy that specializes in behavioural science, put them into action for one of their clients, KFC, the global fast-food brand. KFC saw an opportunity to apply subtle behavioural nudges to guide customer decisions and boost revenue without changing a single product or price. The design team focused on one of the most influential points in the customer journey: the in-store self-order kiosk.

Using a handful of the nudges explored in this chapter, the team ran a 'test and learn' programme to observe how customers responded to subtle shifts in how prices and products were presented. This real-world experiment resulted in increases in customer spend of up to 5%, with the selection of certain strategic products more than doubling. These results highlight the powerful role that presentation plays in shaping decisions and the importance of real-world testing to find the methods best suited to a particular audience in context.

The nudges shared in this chapter show just how powerful price presentation can be. Without changing the price itself, you can influence how customers perceive value and guide their decisions more confidently.

These subtle shifts are low-effort, high-impact, but not one-size-fits-all. What resonates with one audience may not land with another, and subtle factors can make a big difference. For instance, one study found that men perceived a greater discount when the price was shown in red, while the same effect wasn't observed for women.[17] Getting the kind of results KFC saw requires a clear understanding of how your customers respond. Some nudges will hit the mark, while others might fall flat.

Plan Your Next Step

Now it's your turn. Return to your Pricing Prototype, or your current pricing page, proposal or offer, and refine it using the nudges shared in this chapter. What can you simplify, highlight or reframe to make your pricing feel clearer, more compelling and easier to say yes to?

Even small tweaks in how you present prices can dramatically shape how they're perceived. Whether you apply one nudge or five, the goal is the same: to influence decision-making without altering the price itself.

Once you've sharpened your prototype or pricing presentation, you're ready to test how it performs in the real world. The next three chapters will walk you through three practical ways to do just that. First, we'll look at gathering qualitative insights from real customer conversations, followed by survey testing, and finally, live experiments.

We begin with interviews because pricing with confidence starts with empathy. Understanding how your customers think, what they value and what they're willing to pay is the foundation for pricing that resonates and converts.

PRICING PLAYBOOK: NUDGE BEHAVIOURS

Here are ten easy-to-apply pricing psychology nudges to consider when presenting your pricing to customers:

1. **Use small fonts for prices**
   Make prices feel smaller by displaying them in smaller font sizes.

2. **Shorten the visual length of your prices**
   Remove unnecessary commas and decimals to make prices easier to read.

3. **Use charm pricing**
   End prices in a 9 to reduce the left digit by one, making the price feel noticeably lower.

4. **Add social proof**
   Build trust and make decisions easier by showing that others have made the same smart choice.

5. **Anchor with any high number**
   Place a higher number near your price to make your actual price feel more reasonable by comparison.

6. **Show real people**
   Include photos of real customers or team members to build emotional connection and trust.

7. **Reduce choice**
   Keep purchase choices simple and intuitive to make it easier for customers to decide.

8. **Sort prices from high to low**
   List your most expensive option first to make the others feel more affordable.

9. **Reframe the price**
   Break costs into smaller, relatable amounts (e.g. '£3 per day') or present them in the format your customer uses to make decisions, like monthly or annual spend.

10. **Tailor discounts to price points**
    Use % discounts for lower-priced items and absolute £ discounts for higher-priced ones.

Validate

5
TALK TO CUSTOMERS

'The insights from listening to our customers in this way have become the foundation for our strategic direction.'

GURDIP SINGH *CEO, Kallik*

What if simply talking to your customers could unlock the revenue you're leaving on the table?

In most companies, pricing decisions are shaped by internal teams, such as finance, sales and leadership. These teams often assume that they know what customers value and therefore what they will pay. But pricing isn't a one-sided decision. It's an ongoing conversation between your business and your market, and like any meaningful conversation, it requires listening.

Customers evaluate your price based on what they believe they're getting in return. Without their input, you risk setting prices based on assumptions rather than real-world perceptions of value.

In this chapter, we'll go directly to the source. By speaking to your customers and prospects, you'll uncover insights that will transform your pricing strategy. You'll also have the chance to test the prototype you created in Chapter 3 to gather early reactions, uncover blind spots and sharpen your thinking before you make any big moves.

Get to the 'Why' Behind Willingness to Pay

Conversations with customers and prospects can unlock a deep understanding of how they perceive value, what pain points they experience and, ultimately, how much they are willing to pay. These conversations can reveal nuances and 'aha!' moments that change the course of your pricing approach by bridging the gap between what your Pricing Sprint team *think* customers want and what customers *actually* want. By speaking directly to your audience, you're able to test your pricing hypotheses and validate that the value you're offering matches their willingness to pay.

One of the most foundational yet transformative ideas in adopting a customer-led approach to pricing is the concept of Service-Dominant Logic.[1] Think of it as flipping the traditional way of looking at value on its head. Instead of treating value as something delivered at the point of purchase, it's something that customers experience every time they interact with your product or service. It's about the ongoing relationship between what you offer and how it helps your customers succeed, solve problems, or feel good about their choices.

For example, when a customer subscribes to a time-tracking app, the value isn't in making the purchase. It's realized every time they log hours accurately, use reports to make better decisions, or save time on admin. Pricing, in this context, isn't about a single purchase decision; it's part of an ongoing story about the value that your product delivers in real life.

People experience value in many different ways. Research by Bain & Company found 30 different elements of value for Business to Customer (B2C)[2] contexts and 40 elements for Business to Business (B2B).[3] Their 'Elements of Value' model highlights that customers – whether individual or business buyers – seek functional benefits like cost savings, efficiency and reliability. But they also respond strongly to emotional value, such as reducing stress or fostering a sense of trust. Furthermore, intangible elements of value, like social impact or personal achievement, can be critical drivers of purchasing decisions.

Ann has a travel mug from her favourite roaster when she lived in the UK: Coaltown Coffee. Now that she's back in the United States, it reminds her fondly of her time spent in Wales (nostalgia). It keeps her coffee warm, so she brings it with her every time she goes to work from a cafe (functional value). Furthermore, she often receives compliments on the mug, serving as a powerful conversation starter (social value).

Ann's travel mug perfectly illustrates how multiple elements of value come together to shape a customer's perception and willingness to pay. This layered value isn't something that Ann may have articulated upfront – and your customers may not either! But by talking directly with customers, businesses can unearth these rich, intangible benefits that might otherwise be missed.

Understanding how your customers view value across these multifaceted layers allows you to price for what your product *does* and what it *means* to your customers. Entering into customer conversations with this mindset enables you to probe deeper than the functional benefits of your product or service. What emotional or aspirational needs are you fulfilling? Are you helping your customers achieve a life goal or feel connected to something bigger than themselves? The more layers of value you understand, the more you can tailor your pricing strategy to align with how your customers perceive this value.

A time-tracking app for consultants might initially be seen as a functional tool to log hours spent on tasks. However, through customer interviews, the sprint team may discover that its reporting capabilities have helped users make more informed decisions. Digging deeper, they could find that customers have been using the app to improve future project estimates, and over time have increased accuracy by 10%, leading to an additional $2.5m in annual revenue across the firm. This insight highlights new possibilities for their pricing strategy. First, they may have pricing headroom, particularly for super-users who derive significant value. Second, there may be an opportunity to repackage the offering, moving these high-value users into more advanced tiers at higher price points. Refer back to Chapter 3 to learn more about prototypes and offering choice.

Price and value are inextricably linked. While quantitative research methods such as surveys are crucial for understanding value at scale (we'll cover this more in Chapter 6), they often lack the depth to

Price and value are inextricably linked.

capture the full picture of a customer's experience. This is where qualitative research methods such as interviews become indispensable. By engaging directly with customers and prospects, you can uncover the moments when they feel the greatest value, pinpoint the recurring problems that your product solves, and discover which features or services they rely on most. Through these conversations, you gain insights into how much customers are willing to pay and *why* they are willing to pay, enabling a more dynamic and tailored pricing strategy that evolves with the needs and expectations of your market. Without these discussions, you're only guessing at what drives value for your customers.

Theory lesson over. Let's dive into the practicalities of getting direct feedback from customers and prospects to validate (or disprove) your hypotheses and uncover where the real value lies in their experience with your product or service.

Select the Right Interviewees

The insights you gather will be shaped by the perspectives, experiences and backgrounds of the people providing them. If your sample isn't representative of the customers that your Pricing Sprint is designing for, you risk making pricing decisions based on incomplete or skewed data.

Getting feedback from the right mix of people means that your subsequent pricing decisions will reflect market realities, not only the opinions of the easiest-to-reach voices.

This section will guide you through the key choices you need to make when preparing for these conversations.

Choice #1: Who to Talk to

Choosing the right participants helps ensure that your insights come from people with relevant buying context. The three key groups to consider are customers, lost leads and prospects. Each has its advantages, but they also come with distinct trade-offs.

Existing Customers

Your existing customers are a great place to start. They are often the easiest group to reach because they already know your brand, and you have direct access to them.

Including customers in your research is especially valuable because they experience your product or service from a perspective that is uniquely their own. Their first-hand experience gives them a vantage point you simply can't replicate. Talking to them helps you understand how perceptions, needs and value drivers differ across your actual user base.

This familiarity, however, comes with a shadow side. Their past experience will anchor them on established expectations of price, delivery and more. This makes them ideal for understanding retention behaviours, but less useful for uncovering the barriers that stop new customers from converting.

Lost Leads and Lost Customers

Talking to lost leads can help you understand why some potential buyers ultimately chose not to purchase and what solution they chose instead. Re-engaging lost customers offers a view into why someone who initially saw value in your product or service eventually walked away. This group can shed light on unmet needs, pain points or competitor offers that influenced their decision to go elsewhere, whether that's price, service quality, product fit or something else entirely.

Reaching out to lost leads or even lost customers can require extra effort. Get creative by offering incentives to participate and by working with your customer-facing team to craft a thoughtful engagement plan.

Prospects

Speaking with prospects, on the other hand, provides a fresh perspective. Pricing isn't just about those who already buy from you; it's about those who could be buying but aren't yet. By talking to prospects, you can get a clearer picture of how your pricing affects purchasing decisions, what alternatives they're considering, and how your prices stack up against competitors. This can reveal potential barriers to entry, price sensitivity that you may not have spotted with existing customers, or alternative providers that your prospects might be considering.

One way to reach prospects not already in your pipeline is to work with a research recruitment agency. They can help source participants who closely match your target profile, allowing you to hear new perspectives that are not biased by prior familiarity with your brand. Working with a recruiter does come with added cost, but the benefits of accessing potential customers with unbiased perspectives are usually well worth it. In fact, we worked with one FPE Capital portfolio company that was looking to validate willingness to pay before entering the US market, and our research delivered insight *and* opportunity. The interviews we ran with high-value prospects triggered early interest from three potential enterprise leads.

Choice #2: Who Not to Talk to

When it comes to interviews, it's important to keep in mind that talking to certain groups may skew your insights or compromise your sales conversations. That's why being clear about who you won't talk to can be just as important as who you do. Think carefully before engaging the following groups.

People Close to You

Avoid interviewing people who are too close to you, such as family and friends. While they might offer well-intentioned advice, their feedback is often skewed and less valuable for gaining objective pricing insights. This effect is compounded when the person you are talking to doesn't fit the profile of your target customer.

Hot Prospects

Be cautious about including 'hot leads' who are already heavily engaged in the sales process. You want to avoid the risk of unintentionally disrupting the sales conversation, creating confusion about the offering, or introducing concerns they hadn't previously considered. These individuals may also alter their responses based on their interest in your product or their desire to negotiate a better deal, rather than providing neutral, unbiased feedback.

Instead, focus on prospects who match your target profile but are not actively in your sales pipeline. This will help you gather candid, useful insights without interfering with ongoing sales discussions.

If you do wish to involve active prospects in research, collaborate with your sales team to identify appropriate timing and structure so the conversation complements, rather than complicates, their buying journey.

Near-Renewal Customers

Similar to the risks with hot prospects, use caution when engaging customers who are close to renewal. This is especially true in larger, enterprise-level deals, where introducing pricing questions too close to contract renegotiations may create unnecessary doubts or questions that could derail the conversation.

Choice #3: How Many

Deciding how many customers to interview involves striking a balance between depth and efficiency. While speaking with more people could provide a broader range of perspectives, it would also significantly slow down your process. Especially if this type of customer research is new in your organization, it's okay to start small. Aim to interview five customers to get familiar with the interview process and begin to identify recurring patterns and commonalities. After getting these interviews under your belt, you might iterate your approach based on feedback and then interview another five customers to validate the changes you made or decide you have enough new insight to move ahead.

That said, the decision about *which* customers to interview will also determine *how many* interviews you need. If you're just starting out or running a smaller business, casting a wide net can be the best approach. Interviewing a diverse mix of customers across different industries, company sizes or usage scenarios will help you uncover varied perspectives on your pricing model, value delivery and willingness to pay. At this stage, your goal isn't to validate a specific pricing decision but to explore patterns and uncover insights that shape your understanding of who you serve best and, importantly, who you don't.

These early interviews act as a foundation, helping you refine your approach before making bigger pricing decisions. Once you've identified key customer types, you can shift to a more targeted approach, conducting additional interviews within specific segments to validate assumptions and test pricing strategies with the right audience. This ensures that your pricing decisions aren't based on general opinions but on real-world insights from the customers who matter most.

However, if you already serve different customer segments and know these groups have distinct needs, you may want to take a more focused approach from the start. Conducting five to six interviews per segment will allow you to dive deeper into the specific needs, behaviours and pricing expectations of each group. For example, if you are in B2B sales serving both large and small businesses, your enterprise customers might value different features and be willing to pay a premium compared to small businesses. In this case, segmenting your interviews will help you avoid overlooking critical insights unique to each group.

To keep things manageable, focus on only two to three customer segments at a time. This targeted approach enables you to gain deep, actionable insights while keeping the process manageable. By breaking down the task into segments, you can more easily share the load with your team.

Run Exceptional Pricing Interviews

When it comes to pricing, running exceptional interviews is about asking the right questions and extracting actionable insights that directly inform your pricing decisions. Pricing Interviews differ from standard customer feedback sessions because they focus on uncovering perceptions of value, willingness to pay and decision-making processes.

Prepare Materials to Prompt Reactions

Engaging customers or prospects beyond a simple conversation is key to gathering meaningful insights. While interviews begin with dialogue, introducing tools such as concept statements, card sorts or Pricing Prototypes encourages richer, more thoughtful responses. These may be referred to as 'stimuli' or 'artefacts'. However you refer to them, these tangible prompts help people articulate what they value, uncover expectations and surface insights that may otherwise remain hidden.

Concept Statements

High-level positioning statements or a two- to three-minute introduction video are especially useful when interviewing participants unfamiliar with your brand. These statements enable you to gauge the clarity and relevance of your messaging. They help you understand how well your brand and value proposition resonate, while grounding the interviewee in what you are about to discuss.

Card Sort

A card sort uses a set of prepared physical or virtual cards, each representing a feature or benefit. Participants sort and prioritize these cards into categories to highlight what matters most and least to them. This process provides a clear visual hierarchy of customer priorities, revealing which features and benefits resonate most strongly. By understanding these preferences, you can more effectively structure your pricing tiers and product roadmap.

Pricing Prototypes

Mock-ups or detailed visuals of different pricing options allow interviewees to react to specific tier structures, feature bundles or price points, giving you direct insights into their pricing sensitivities and perceived value. Return to Chapter 3 for more on designing a Pricing Prototype.

As you prepare your prototype to be shared in a Pricing Interview, think about what you are looking to learn. In some cases, it's helpful to start by sharing an unpriced version. This allows you to learn about reactions to the offer first, then ask about willingness to pay without anchoring the interviewee on a suggested price point. You can then introduce a priced version to compare responses to pre-prepared prices and understand how it aligns with their original expectations.

Discussion Guide

Concept statements, card sorts and Pricing Prototypes help you move beyond surface opinions to uncover the real drivers behind what customers value and what they're willing to pay for. However, using them at the right time in the interview matters. That's where your discussion guide comes in.

A discussion guide is your script for running effective interviews. It outlines how you'll open the conversation, the key topics you'll explore and the open-ended questions you'll ask. It also includes prompts for any stimulus you plan to show, and a rough sense of timing to help you stay on track.

A well-crafted discussion guide helps you run a semi-structured interview where you have the space and flexibility to follow new insights while keeping your core objectives front and centre.

Let's look at how to structure the interview step by step.

Structure Your Interview

Conducting Pricing Interviews is an integral part of the Pricing Sprints we run with our clients. By working as a neutral third party, we eliminate biases that might come from being too close to the product or idea. This separation between the business and interviewer allows us to ask tough, unbiased questions that elicit honest responses, even from the most reserved interviewees. This approach means that our interviews yield insights to directly inform robust, customer-centred pricing decisions.

An effective Pricing Interview strikes a delicate balance between being overprepared and understructured.

An effective Pricing Interview strikes a delicate balance between being overprepared and understructured. Preparation ensures that you address all key areas, while a flexible structure helps you listen deeply and explore unexpected avenues of insight. We've found that this combination uncovers the most valuable insights.

Whether your Pricing Sprint team decides to conduct these interviews internally or partner with expert researchers, investing time and care into understanding customer perceptions is one of the most powerful steps you can take towards confident pricing. If you choose to run the interviews internally, consider sharing the task of interviewing across your sprint team, as this has the added benefit of building buy-in from key stakeholders. When key players are part of the process, they're more likely to support and advocate for the resulting decisions, knowing they have been shaped by the voice of real customers.

We find that many participants say this is the most memorable and meaningful part of a Pricing Sprint, especially for senior leaders who may rarely have the chance to speak directly with customers. Rolling up their sleeves to listen firsthand can be both eye-opening and unexpectedly enjoyable, bringing a renewed sense of clarity and purpose to the pricing work ahead. If you have an established internal research team, consider scheduling interviews so each member of the sprint team can observe at least one live interview.

In this chapter, we focus on interviews through the lens of pricing. We'll cover how to ask direct questions about price and value that generate meaningful, honest responses, but we won't dive into the deeper theory behind interviewing, techniques for managing bias, or ethics. While these are essential for running insightful, inclusive interviews, there are already excellent resources available for those new to qualitative research.*

Great Pricing Interviews are approached in a semi-structured way that allows you to balance structure with flexibility. The following six phases will help you do just that. You'll gather the deep insights you need while keeping the conversation open and exploratory so you can learn things you didn't expect along the way.

Open

How you open sets the tone for the rest of the interview. Start by introducing yourself and explaining the purpose of the interview. This is your opportunity to make the participant feel at ease and understand what is expected of them. Let them know that their honest feedback is valuable and there are no right or wrong answers. Keep this part light and reassuring as it builds rapport and encourages openness from the participant.

---

*If you're new to interviewing customers, we recommend the book *The Mom Test*. It's an easy read and serves as a simple yet effective guide for asking questions that generate meaningful and honest responses.[4]

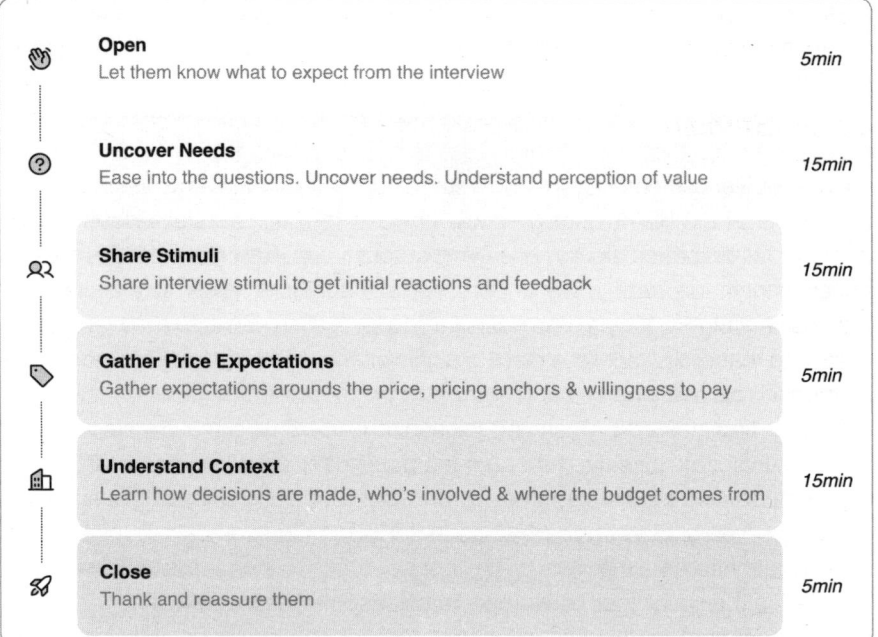

Figure 5.1 Pricing Interview structure.

Uncover Needs

Uncover the interviewee's needs and their perception of value. Begin by using broad questions to understand their background, usage patterns, and overall experience with your or similar products or services. The key is gathering insights into the challenges that customers face and what they value before introducing any of the concepts or prototypes you want to test.

Use open-ended questions here. Encourage them to share their thoughts freely while you listen actively. Avoid jumping into pricing or product specifics just yet. Instead, focus on understanding their problems and how they approach solving them.

Here are six key questions to get you started:

1. Can you walk me through how you do . . . [the process]?
2. What are some of the biggest challenges you experience along the way?
3. How are you managing [the challenge] now?
4. Can you share an example of the last time you . . . [current challenge/solution]?
5. What else have you considered to solve . . . [the challenge]?

6. How important is solving [challenge x] compared to solving [challenge y that you also mentioned]?

Share Stimuli

Once you've gained a solid understanding of your interviewee's needs and context, the next step is to move from general discussion to targeted exploration. Here, you'll introduce the specific stimuli you've prepared. As mentioned earlier, these can range from a concept statement or a card-sorting exercise to a detailed Pricing Prototype. The goal of using such materials is to show something concrete that elicits real-time reactions, allowing you to observe your customers' immediate perceptions, aversions and delights.

Presenting something tangible during an interview lets you step beyond hypothetical questions and into how the participant actually feels about specific options. Watch for facial expressions, body language and moments of silence as these non-verbal cues can reveal just as much as the spoken responses.

Pay attention to the words they choose. If they describe something as 'confusing', 'too busy' or 'straightforward', this is a window into their experience and can highlight which elements resonate or need adjustment. If an interviewee is hesitant or vague, gently prompt them to dig deeper. Simple follow-ups such as 'Why is that?' or 'Tell me more about . . .' can unveil underlying beliefs, experiences and motivations, helping you uncover the real drivers of decision-making.

Gather Price Expectations

Now that you've explored needs, perceptions, and initial reactions to your concepts, it's time to dive into price expectations. This phase of the interview helps you establish a clearer sense of willingness to pay, gauge price sensitivity and understand how they perceive the value of your offering.

Even for experienced researchers, discussing price can feel like navigating a minefield. Money is a deeply personal and sometimes uncomfortable topic, but it's also one of the most valuable areas to explore. By approaching these conversations with confidence and a bit of structure, you can uncover critical insights that inform your pricing strategy.

We use an adapted version of the Van Westendorp questions to ask about price. The Van Westendorp Price Sensitivity Meter is a well-established tool in pricing research for understanding what customers consider a reasonable price. The model is most commonly used in a quantitative setting where data from four key questions about price enables you to plot a statistically acceptable price range and optimal price point. Chapter 6 introduces the quantitative version of the Van Westendorp Price Sensitivity Meter. For qualitative interviews, we simplify the model to two key questions:

1. 'At what price would you consider this to be great value for money?'

2. 'At what price would this be getting expensive but you might still consider it?'

These questions reveal the lower and upper bounds of an acceptable price for the interviewee, based on their current perceptions. This provides far greater explanatory power than a simple question of 'How much are you willing to pay?'

Our research team regularly uses these questions to gain insights into pricing on a wide range of products and services, from everyday consumer goods to six-figure enterprise software solutions. However, the value of these questions in a qualitative setting lies more in the conversations they generate than in the specific numbers they surface. Interview responses tell us the *why* behind the number, while the Pricing Survey that follows in Chapter 6 provides the actual numbers at a level of statistical significance needed to make confident pricing decisions.

Price expectations tend to be more reliable when evaluating products or services that customers can easily compare to existing benchmarks. A prospective customer for Pour & Prosper Coffee Co. is likely have a mental pricing framework shaped by experiences ranging from budget-friendly grocery store beans to high-end roastery subscriptions. This familiarity allows them to provide a relatively accurate response to questions like 'At what price would you consider this a great value for the money?' By conducting multiple interviews, patterns will emerge, offering clarity on whether your pricing aligns with customer expectations and sits within the acceptable range.

For larger, more complex purchases, engaging customers in discussions about price expectations requires a more exploratory approach. Instead of aiming for pinpoint accuracy on specific price points, focus on uncovering the mental maths that customers use to evaluate the cost of a solution like yours. This involves understanding their pricing anchors – the reference points or benchmarks that shape their perception of value.

To guide the discussion, ask 'At what price would you consider this to be great value for the money?' Then follow up with questions to understand the context:

- 'Can you walk me through how you came up with that number?'
- 'Would you expect to pay that one time, monthly, annually, or something else?'

As customers respond, listen carefully and follow up with clarifying questions to probe deeper into their reasoning. For example, if they mention preferring a subscription model, ask why that structure appeals to them. Their answer might reveal preferences for operational expenses, ongoing support or contract terms.

On the other hand, if they reference a one-time investment, it could indicate they're comparing your solution to an upfront purchase with no intention of an ongoing relationship.

Once you've explored these open-ended pricing expectations, you can also show the specific price points you are considering to gauge their reactions. This progression from asking to showing often sparks richer discussions. It can uncover whether their initial estimates align with reality, expose pain points in your pricing structure, or highlight opportunities to better communicate value.

To bring this to life, let's look at the sustainability startup from Chapter 2. They were working in such a nascent market that their customers had very few purchase experiences they could draw on to determine what they would view as a 'great value' or 'getting expensive'. Therefore the pricing question used during interviews yielded a wide range of price expectations, from comparisons to a double-digit Netflix subscription to much larger six-digit enterprise-level spends.

Customers often lack familiar reference points when testing pricing for emerging categories or new technology. For the sprint team, this meant one thing: they needed to play an active role in shaping how value was understood. Educating their audience and anchoring price expectations would be essential. It also highlighted the need to think in segments. Different customers saw different levels of value and had different willingness to pay. Rather than setting a single price, the team began exploring a tiered approach to better match each group's needs and budget.

Whatever the focus of your Pricing Sprint, the key takeaway is that conversations like these go far beyond pinpointing a number. They reveal how people make decisions, what they're really comparing you to, and where you might have room to grow. These are the kind of insights that lead to pricing strategies that truly fit the way your customers want to buy.

Understand Context

To truly understand willingness to pay, you need to explore the context in which customers make purchasing decisions. This includes who is involved, what influences their choices and how they evaluate options. By understanding these dynamics, you can craft a pricing strategy that aligns more effectively with their buying process and priorities.

Here are some key questions to uncover the decision-making context:

B2B Interviews	B2C Interviews	Listen For
What else would you need to consider before purchasing this?	What else would you want to know before buying this?	Listen for questions or concerns that might delay or impact the buying decision.
Who else would be involved?*e.g. other stakeholders in the organization*	Who else would be involved in your decision to purchase this? *e.g. friends, parents or partner*	Listen for who might influence or make the final decision. This allows you to anticipate objections and tailor messaging to a range of stakeholders.
Where would the budget come from?	How much have you spent on [category] in the last month/year?	Listen for where the budget comes from and any constraints. This helps you align your offering with their financial priorities.
How would you measure ROI?	How would this change _____?	Listen for their criteria for success and insight into how they define value. This enables you to frame your pricing in terms of outcomes they prioritize.
Are there any other solutions you are considering in this space?	What are the alternatives you are considering?	Listen for competitors and alternatives. This helps you position your product effectively among a range of viable alternatives.
How likely are you to consider a solution like this in the next [timeframe]? Why/why not?	How likely are you to buy _____ in the next [timeframe]? Why/why not?	Listen for their readiness to buy. This helps you qualify responses from those with the highest intent to purchase.
When was the last time you purchased a solution like this? Tell me about it.	When was the last time you bought _____? Tell me about it.	Listen for differences in what they say they would do in the last question and what they have actually done in the past.

Figure 5.2 Pricing Interview questions.

Exploring context helps you move beyond the price tag to other factors shaping your customer's decision-making. Whether it's understanding who has the final say or identifying constraints like timelines or competing budgets, this insight enables you to design pricing strategies that resonate with their reality. It also helps you uncover the true role that price plays in the decision. By understanding the bigger picture, you ensure that your pricing is strategically aligned with how your customers think, decide and act.

Close

As the interview comes to a close, it's important to leave your participant feeling appreciated and valued. More often than not, customers or prospects are pleased to share their opinions, and the final moments of the conversation are the perfect opportunity to reinforce their contribution and thank them for their time.

Steps to close effectively:

1. **Invite them to share anything they might not have had the chance to mention.**
   This gives them a final opportunity to add insights or ideas they may have overlooked during the conversation. Ask 'Is there anything else you'd like to share that we didn't cover today?'

2. **Thank them personally.**
   Referencing something specific reinforces the value they added and shows that you were actively listening. Say something like 'I really appreciated your thoughts on [specific feedback],' or 'Your perspective on [insight] was especially helpful,' or 'The way you [specific behaviour] really helped [specific result].'

3. **Let them know what to expect moving forward.**
   For example, if an incentive was offered for their participation, share something like 'We'll be sending out [specific incentive, e.g. a gift card] by [specific timeframe].'

4. **End on a high note.**
   Emphasize the impact of their contribution by saying something like 'Your input today will play a big role in helping us create a better experience for customers like you. Thank you again for your time and thoughtful feedback.'

Closing with warmth and professionalism makes your interviewee feel heard and valued, and leaves a positive impression that strengthens their connection to your business.

Analyse What You Have Learned

It's tempting to act on fresh insights immediately after an interview, especially when they feel clear and actionable. However, beware of recency bias, a psychological effect that makes recent experiences more vivid and memorable than earlier ones. This can lead to placing undue weight on the most recent interview insights simply because they are freshest in your mind.

Take the time to step back and reflect deeply on what you've learned across all interviews. Look for patterns and start to connect the dots. It is through a careful analysis that you will form a coherent picture of your customers' needs, perceptions and decision-making processes.

To structure your analysis effectively and align it with specific decisions, start by reviewing your interview transcripts to extract key responses. Look for statements that directly relate to your core questions or hypotheses, highlighting them for easy reference.

A helpful technique is to create a summary view that systematically captures these key insights across all interviews. Consider using a colour-coded system to group similar themes, such as pain points, desired outcomes or price sensitivity. You can use a spreadsheet, sticky notes or a dedicated research platform. Whichever method works best for you, the key is to identify patterns objectively and ensure that no single interview dominates your perspective.

Once you've organized the data, look for patterns that connect directly to the pricing decisions you need to make. For instance, if you're evaluating whether to offer a free trial, focus on responses that reveal customer expectations when trying a new product, such as how long they need to experience the product's value, or what might hold them back from converting to a paid plan afterwards. Similarly, when assessing a pricing model such as subscription vs. pay-per-use, listen for commonalities in the preferences, hesitations or competitor comparisons you hear. Rather than being swayed by one-off comments, pay attention to themes that emerge across multiple interviews. If a pricing concern is mentioned by more than half of the participants, it's more likely to be a real customer priority rather than an isolated opinion.

Let's consider a food delivery service that is looking to inform some critical pricing decisions. Figure 5.3 captures common themes from customer interviews, then maps them to each pricing decision, helping their team extract clear, actionable insights that drive confident pricing action.

Hold discussions with your team to help identify key themes. These shared moments of reflection create alignment and enrich your collective understanding of the customer. Once you've distilled the key insights, consider creating a

Pricing Decision	Recurring Theme	Customer Quote	Next Step
Should we offer a free trial?	Customers feel uncertain about value until they experience the product firsthand.	*'I wasn't sure if it was worth the price until I tried it.'*	Test a 14-day vs. 30-day trial length.
How long should a free trial be?	Most customers say they need at least 2–3 weeks to fully evaluate the product.	*'I needed a few weeks to really see the value.'*	Consider a longer trial (e.g. 21–30 days) or a usage-based limit rather than time-based.
Subscription vs. pay-per-use: what's preferred?	Customers prefer subscriptions for predictable costs and ease of budgeting, rather than having to think about payments each time.	*'I just want to set it up once and not have to think about payments every month.'*	Reinforce the benefits of subscription (e.g. 'set and forget' convenience)
What influences willingness to pay?	Customers are willing to pay more for healthy offerings	*'I'd rather pay a bit more for something that's actually good for me.'*	Review product selection and messaging before increasing prices.
How do customers compare us to alternatives?	Competitors with lower entry pricing attract attention, but customers see our advanced features as a differentiator.	*'Other services I've tried are cheaper, but they lack [key feature].'*	Highlight differentiators in pricing tiers. Test a lower entry-level tier.
Should we offer a discount for longer commitments?	Many customers prefer to pay annually if there's a meaningful discount.	*'I would pay for a full year if it meant that I would save money in the long run.'*	Test uptake of annual vs. monthly pricing with a small discount (e.g. 10–15%)

Figure 5.3 Pricing Interview themes.

highlight reel of clips or quotes to share internally.* This keeps the customer's voice central to your decision-making.

---

*Building your own central research repository allows you to revisit past interviews and continue adding new ones over time. Research and insight platforms that include AI features can help find themes quickly and create highlight reels for easy sharing.

Plan Your Next Step

'We have been scared of increasing prices, but the interviews built even stronger, trusted relationships with our customers because we brought them into the process.'

WENDY SCHOEMAN *Head of Client Success, Hermann*

We can't say this enough: pricing is not only about numbers, it's about people. Truly listening to your customers and prospects offers insights into your proposition, product and pricing that data analytics and market reports can't.

If you haven't already, it's time to talk to your customers, prospects or lost leads. Use the techniques in this chapter to guide your conversations. Every interview is a step closer to confident, optimized pricing.

In the next chapter, we'll show you how to take what you learn in these one-to-one conversations and find out if the patterns you've uncovered hold true across your wider market.

PRICING PLAYBOOK: TALK TO CUSTOMERS

Follow these six steps to learn what customers really think about your pricing:

1. Select the Right Interviewees

Prioritize customers, prospects and lost leads who reflect real buying decisions.

2. Prepare materials to prompt reactions

Go beyond conversation by sharing concept statements, card sorts or Pricing Prototypes to uncover what truly matters and what interview participants are willing to pay for.

3. Structure your interview

Design a clear conversation flow that balances consistency with flexibility. Plan your questions in advance, but stay open to where the conversation leads.

4. Run an exceptional Pricing Interview

Create a safe space for honesty, ask open questions, and dig into the 'why' behind their perceptions of price and value.

5. **Gather price expectations**

   Ask specific, structured questions that reveal what customers would happily pay, what feels expensive, and how they think about value in context.

6. **Analyse what you learn**

   Look for patterns across interviews and surface insights to inform your pricing decisions.

6
VALIDATE AT SCALE

You've gathered rich insights from customer interviews, uncovered what drives purchasing decisions, and learned more about what customers truly value and where they see friction in your current offering.

Your next question to answer is: do these insights hold true across your entire market?

It's one thing to hear a handful of customers expressing a strong preference for a particular pricing model or highlight a key value driver. It's another to know whether those sentiments are widespread enough to shape your strategy. That's where a Pricing Survey comes in. Where an interview allows you to reach a handful of people, a Pricing Survey extends to hundreds or even thousands of customers, enabling you to establish a representative view across a complete market.

Blending qualitative (interviews) and quantitative (surveys) research is the gold standard for pricing. The interviews uncover the *how* and *why*, and a Pricing Survey measures *who* and *how many*. When combined, they provide a rock-solid foundation for setting prices with confidence.

> **The interviews uncover the *how* and *why*, and a Pricing Survey measures *who* and *how many*.**

In this chapter, we'll look at how to design a Pricing Survey that will help your Pricing Sprint team validate your insights on price and value at scale. You'll learn how to select the ideal survey respondents, craft compelling requests to participate, design an impactful survey, integrate critical pricing techniques, and effectively analyse the results to derive actionable insights.

Invest in a Pricing Survey

A team of ambitious entrepreneurs came to us as they were preparing to launch a bold new vision for beauty. Their startup, Humanoid Labs, promised to reshape how people interacted with cosmetics by bridging digital and physical products in a way the industry had never seen before.

But there was a problem.

Humanoid was not entering an existing market with clear competitors and well-established pricing benchmarks. There was no dominant player to position themselves against. Instead, they were creating something entirely new, a category that didn't exist yet.

With no playbook to follow, no direct competitors to price against and no established industry norms to use as a guide, how could they decide what to charge?

If the price was too high, potential customers would be alienated before they had a chance to experience the product. If it was too low, they might undermine the very value they were trying to create with their premium yet accessible, high-tech beauty experience.

It wasn't just a pricing question. It was a positioning question.

Our research team designed a two-part survey to uncover the answers.

First, we launched a Segmentation Survey to define Humanoid's true addressable market. With no existing competitors to benchmark against, the team had to build customer segments from the ground up. These segments were not based solely on demographics but on product appeal and willingness to pay.

Armed with these insights, our qualitative research team conducted a series of in-depth interviews with potential customers who had shown high interest in the brand. These conversations helped refine product bundles and a potential pricing framework.*

The Pricing Survey came next and was tailored to their highest-opportunity segments, those where appeal and willingness to pay intersected most strongly. We used this survey to test the qualitative research findings at scale, determining acceptable price ranges and validating the optimal product bundles.

It's one thing to sit across from a customer and hear them say, 'I'd pay more for this.' It's another thing to know, with certainty, that thousands of people feel the same way. In fact, the team learned that their addressable market was twenty times bigger than they had assumed and customers were willing to pay 50% more than originally expected. Not to mention, considering pricing well before launch gave Humanoid a leg up on meeting future revenue targets, something that only 28% of startups achieve.[2]

The results reshaped their entire go-to-market strategy. Feature bundling, product positioning and even investor pitches got stronger based on hard data, not guesswork.

This is why investing in a Pricing Survey is worth it.

---

*For more on methods for designing the product around the price, check out the book *Monetizing Innovation*.[1]

A well-designed Pricing Survey doesn't just confirm whether a price is too high or too low. It's a strategic tool for honing in on how your market perceives value, what drives purchasing decisions, and where the greatest opportunities exist to optimize pricing, positioning and profitability.

Whether you choose to run your Pricing Survey internally or partner with expert researchers, investing time and care into validating your assumptions and testing at scale is one of the most powerful steps you can take towards pricing with confidence, just like Humanoid did.

Design an Exceptional Pricing Survey

In the last chapter, you learned how to run exceptional Pricing Interviews. These are moderated conversations where someone is there to guide the flow, dig deeper and follow unexpected twists. The goal is depth – to understand how people think, feel and make decisions.

With a Pricing Survey, no one is there to guide the respondent. The quality of insights you get back depends on the questions you ask, and you only get one shot to ask them. Designing an exceptional Pricing Survey is about structure, scale and patterns. You are capturing responses from a larger group to spot trends and make confident, data-led decisions.

A Pricing Survey is much more than your run-of-the-mill customer feedback form. It reveals the nuanced perceptions of value, willingness to pay and decision-making processes that underpin pricing success.

An exceptional Pricing Survey asks the *right* questions in the *right* way. The secret lies in keeping respondents engaged while gathering insights that go beyond surface-level preferences. The interview materials you created in Chapter 5 (such as concept statements, card sorts and Pricing Prototypes) can also be adapted for use in a Pricing Survey to make the survey experience more interactive, nudging participants to think critically about what they value and why.

For example, you may be tempted to ask 'Would you pay $50 for this?' Instead, you might present a Pricing Prototype – first tested and iterated after a set of Pricing Interviews – that includes three different packages. In this case, you would ask 'Which package best suits you?', followed by a carefully structured set of questions to uncover what they would expect to pay for their chosen package and what trade-offs they'd consider at different price points.

This approach does more than just collect numbers; it mimics real-world decision-making. Instead of forcing respondents to estimate a hypothetical price, it reveals how they weigh options, what features drive value, and where pricing thresholds naturally emerge. These techniques also fend off the dreaded survey fatigue, keeping participants engaged and providing richer, more reliable insights even when you're not in the room.

Here's what makes a Pricing Survey truly exceptional:

- **Be intentional.** Every question should tie directly to a pricing decision you need to make or a hypothesis you are looking to test. See Chapter 1 for more on drafting hypotheses.

- **Remove guesswork.** Avoid vague or subjective questions. Instead, provide structured scenarios or choices that lead to clear, actionable answers.

- **Engage like a storyteller.** Just as a good story keeps its audience hooked, your survey should guide respondents on a journey that feels purposeful and relevant, not tedious.

Think of your Pricing Survey as an investment. Done right, it doesn't just inform pricing; it builds a foundation for marketing, product development and customer relationships. When you truly understand what makes your customers tick, you are doing more than setting prices; you're shaping your business for growth.

Here's what we heard from one brand director after seeing Pricing Survey results: *"My mind is whirling. It backs up some of our hypotheses and informs our direction of travel. Great to see what people react to and engage with, and what value they put against that. So many insights to digest and take away and inform what we do next."*

Keep in mind that if you lack the in-house expertise to design an exceptional Pricing Survey, partnering with an experienced quantitative researcher can be a smart move. A specialist can not only help design and execute a Pricing Survey that delivers reliable results, they can also ensure a rigorous and independent analysis of the results.

Identify the Purpose

Every Pricing Survey should be designed with a clear purpose: to answer specific questions that directly inform your pricing strategy. Without this clarity, surveys risk collecting data that is interesting but ultimately unhelpful when making decisions. The best way to be confident that your survey delivers actionable insights is to work backwards from the pricing decisions you need to make.

For example, if you're considering setting your prices deliberately above or below key competitors, your survey needs to confirm whether customers actively compare prices before purchasing. Simply asking 'How important is price to you?' isn't enough. Instead, dig deeper with questions like 'Which brands or alternatives did you consider before purchasing?', 'Which did you purchase from last?' and 'Which factors influenced your decision to choose X for your last purchase?' If customers aren't actively comparing prices, then setting your price in direct relation to competitors may not be as critical as you assumed. If they are, you'll also need to understand which competitors they're benchmarking against and how much weight the price carries versus other decision factors like brand, convenience or product features. This enables you to base your pricing decisions on real customer behaviour rather than guesswork.

Similarly, when developing a good-better-best pricing structure, the survey should reveal whether customers naturally segment into different groups based on their willingness to pay. One way to test this is by presenting different competing offers and asking respondents which option best meets their needs. If most customers gravitate towards the lowest-priced option, you may need to strengthen the perceived value of your higher-priced offers. If the responses are evenly spread, it suggests that your offering is well-aligned with customer preferences.

A well-structured survey provides insights into what customers will pay, how they evaluate price, what tradeoffs they are willing to make, and how they compare different pricing options. When designed with the end decision in mind, surveys become powerful tools for shaping your pricing strategy.

Decide Between a Branded or Blind Survey

Surveys can be branded (the respondent knows the company they are responding to) or blind (the name company is hidden). The decision between branded or blind depends on the insights you need, how you want respondents to approach their answers, and who you are inviting to participate.

Branded Surveys

Branded surveys work well when gathering feedback from existing customers as the connection to your company builds trust and encourages thoughtful responses. Customers are more likely to engage if they recognize your name and understand that their feedback could influence future pricing decisions.

There are two things to keep in mind if you are considering a branded survey. First, be mindful of the bias they introduce. Respondents may answer more favourably to avoid criticizing a brand they like or be overly negative if they've had a bad experience. Second, consider the level of risk the contents of the survey may pose to your brand. If you're sharing a Pricing Prototype or testing a new concept, think carefully about how it could be interpreted. In highly price-sensitive markets or among customers quick to share feedback publicly via forums or social media, you may unintentionally spark confusion or concern. When in doubt, consider using a blind survey or conducting initial testing with a smaller, trusted group first.

Blind Surveys

Blind surveys are particularly valuable when testing willingness to pay. Without a specific brand clearly sponsoring the survey, responses are more likely to reflect respondents' true perceptions of value and pricing expectations of the product or service, independent of brand. Blind surveys are also the ideal option in highly price-sensitive markets and for those who are concerned customers will spread the word about something in the survey.

Working with a research sample provider who distributes surveys on your behalf can help to keep the survey brand-neutral.

Hybrid Surveys

Plot twist: your survey doesn't have to be only branded or only blind; a hybrid approach can also be effective.

For example, a Pricing Survey might be anonymous when sent to prospective customers to get an unbiased view of market needs and price sensitivity. You may then send the same survey to an existing customer database with branded messaging to invite feedback from people who already know and trust your business.

The benefit of this hybrid approach is the ability to analyse both data sets independently, then compare results across groups. It also helps you see how brand familiarity and customer experience influence perceptions of value and willingness to pay.

Select the Right Survey Respondents

In addition to asking the right *questions*, the job of an exceptional Pricing Survey is to ask the right questions to the right *people*. Pricing Survey respondents should accurately represent your target market. Selecting the right audience means that the data reflects real buying behaviours, not just opinions from those who may never consider your product.

Generally, the same rules apply as those you used to select the right participants for Pricing Interviews in Chapter 5. However, when it comes to surveys, there are three important differences to keep in mind: sample size, representation, and quality control.

Sample Size

Surveys require far more responses than interviews to be meaningful. While a handful of in-depth conversations can uncover powerful insights in qualitative research, Pricing Surveys rely on patterns and relationships that confidently emerge only with sufficient numbers.

If you're targeting a larger market, but don't have direct access to a big enough sample or want to reach a prospective market, you may want to work with a third-party research sample provider. These partners can source participants that match your target customer profile, allowing you to gather responses at scale and improve data quality.

If your audience is small or hard to reach, gathering enough responses to ensure the statistical validity of your survey can be challenging. For example, if you serve a niche group such as government buyers or C-suite executives in a specialized industry, a survey may still be feasible, with targeted recruitment, but a large-scale survey may not be practical. In these cases, qualitative interviews (covered in Chapter 5) remain your most reliable tool and can be supplemented with pricing experiments (Chapter 7).

Representation

Even with a large sample, you need to have the right *mix* of respondents. For example, if your target market is evenly split between two industry sectors, but 80% of your survey responses come from just one of them, your results will be skewed. Similarly, if you serve both budget-conscious and premium customers, your survey should reflect both groups proportionally.

Use demographic or behavioural quotas to help balance your sample and be sure that your data reflects the diversity of your target market. Research sample providers can help you set and monitor these quotas to find a representative data set.

Quality Control

Finally, inviting the right *respondents* to answer the right *questions* still isn't quite enough for an exceptional Pricing Survey. You need to make sure the responses you get back are *reliable*.

Low-effort responses can dilute your insights and reduce the credibility of your findings. Watch out for signs that respondents are rushing through just to finish, such as clicking in the same place every time or completing it suspiciously quickly. This is most common for blind, high-volume online surveys that incentivize participation.

To protect against this, build some basic attention-check questions into your survey, monitor for unrealistic completion speeds, and scan for obviously inattentive response patterns. Open-text questions can also act as a simple filter, with nonsensical or obviously AI-generated answers being a clear red flag.

If you're using a sample provider, ask how they screen for low-quality or fraudulent responses. Most reputable providers have internal quality assurance processes, but it's worth making sure.

Frame the Request to Participate

Now that you've identified the right mix of respondents to gather meaningful pricing insights, the next challenge is getting them to engage. Even the most well-designed survey is only valuable if people actually respond.

How you invite participants can make the difference between a strong data-rich study and a low response rate that leaves gaps in your insights. A well-crafted request means that your audience understands why their input matters, feels motivated to participate and trusts that their time will be well spent.

A well-crafted request means that your audience understands why their input matters.

Use this checklist to make your survey invitations are clear, engaging and designed to maximize participation:

- **Be authentic.** For branded surveys, check that your message aligns with your brand's tone and voice.

- **Be concise.** Keep it short and to the point. Link to additional details where needed.

- **Explain the purpose.** Clearly communicate why you're conducting the survey and how their input will be used.

- **Set expectations.** Let them know how long the survey will take, when the deadline is, and whether their responses will remain anonymous.

- **Highlight incentives.** If you're offering an incentive – such as a gift card, donation or entry into a prize draw – make it clear. Avoid any incentives that relate to your product directly (e.g. a discount on their next purchase) to comply with Market Research Society (MSR) rules that prohibit incentives requiring the respondent to spend money to redeem.

It also ensures unbiased participation, as you want to hear from unhappy customers as much as those likely to repurchase.

- **Share the impact.** Emphasize how their feedback will directly influence decisions and improve their future experience.

Here's an example of a clear and compelling participation request for a branded survey:

Subject: Share your thoughts on [PRODUCT] for a chance to win [INCENTIVE]

Hi [First Name],

At [COMPANY], we are dedicated to improving [VALUE PROPOSITION]. We need your feedback to help shape future improvements, from product features to customer support.

Take the survey now >

The survey should take no more than 10 minutes to complete, depending on your answers. At the end, you can choose to be entered in a prize draw to win [INCENTIVE].

The survey is being run by our specialist external research partner. It's anonymous and completely confidential – nothing you say will be linked to you in any of the data analysis, and there will be no sales follow-up from us or anyone else.

Thanks, as we couldn't do this without you!

[NAME / COMPANY]

Structure Your Pricing Survey

Unlike a face-to-face conversation, a survey doesn't allow follow-up questions or clarifications. That means that every question needs to be clear, intentional and easy to interpret. A well-structured Pricing Survey should follow a logical flow, guiding respondents from broad value perception questions to specific pricing sensitivities.

It's always advisable to pre-test your survey with a small group before launching it to catch any unclear wording, ensure smooth navigation and refine the flow.

Figure 6.1 shares a recommended survey flow to help you design a survey that maximizes engagement and delivers meaningful results.

Survey Section	Purpose	Example Questions
Introduction and screener	Make sure respondents fit the target audience and screen out participants who don't qualify	Which of these best describes your role? or Have you purchased a [category] product in the last 6 months?
Value perception	Understand what customers prioritize before mentioning the price	How important is X/Y/Z when choosing a [product/service]?
Competitor context	Assess whether customers shop around and who they compare you to	Which of the following brands have you considered for this type of purchase?
Price sensitivity and willingness to pay	Identify optimal pricing ranges using tested methodologies	(See Van Westendorp and Gabor-Granger, in the next section.)
Segment differences	Capture variations in needs, value perception and price sensitivity	Which of the following best describes how you use [product/service]?
Demographics and behavioural data	Ensure that findings can be analysed by key segments	What best describes your industry? or What is your annual household income?

Figure 6.1 Pricing Survey flow.

Choose Your Methods

You can take advantage of different methods across your survey depending on what you need to learn. Defining an acceptable price range, pinpointing the optimal price for revenue growth, or understanding what customers value most will each require a different method.

Let's explore three key methodologies: Van Westendorp, Gabor-Granger, MaxDiff.

- **Van Westendorp** is particularly useful for early-stage pricing, especially for innovative or unfamiliar products where customers don't have strong pre-existing price expectations. It helps define an acceptable price range.

- **Gabor-Granger** is ideal for fine-tuning existing pricing models, particularly when there's already an established price benchmark; it allows businesses to pinpoint the exact price that balances sales volume and revenue.

- **MaxDiff** (Maximum Difference Scaling) is a great choice when you need to understand which product features or benefits your customers value most. Rather than focusing purely on price, MaxDiff helps identify what actually drives purchasing decisions, ensuring that your pricing reflects what matters most to your customers.

Even if you plan to outsource your Pricing Survey, understanding these techniques will help you ask the right questions and understand how the results inform your strategic pricing decisions.

Why 'how much would you pay?' is the wrong question

Imagine you're taking part in a survey about a new premium, experimental coffee that Pour & Prosper Coffee Co. is preparing to launch. The description paints a picture of something truly exceptional: a limited release crafted from rare, single-estate microlot beans, ethically sourced, and roasted to order on a restricted schedule. This isn't your everyday brew. It's the kind of coffee you'd expect to find at a specialty tasting event or shared with reverence in the home of a true coffee connoisseur. Then, you reach the key question:

How much would you pay for a bag of this coffee?

A blank text box stares back at you. You hesitate. If you put $39, will that become the actual price? If you go for $18, does that suggest it's only average quality? You find yourself second-guessing, what's the *right* answer? Without clear guidance, you're left balancing between guesswork and self-protection, unsure whether to be honest or strategic. You're not alone. This uncertainty is exactly why open-ended pricing questions often fail in surveys.

Many businesses assume that the simplest way to gauge price is to ask customers directly. However, this is one of the least reliable ways to measure willingness to pay. Why?

1. **People don't think about pricing in a vacuum**
   Customers don't make purchase decisions based purely on an internal, pre-existing price point. They compare, evaluate and react to the way pricing is framed.

2. **They don't want to 'overpay'**
   In a survey, respondents often lowball their answer, not because they wouldn't pay more in real life, but because they don't want to artificially inflate the price.
3. **Conversational price expectations don't match real-world behaviour**
   Just because someone *says* they'd only pay $18 for a bag of coffee doesn't mean they won't spend $39 impulsively on a highly exclusive purchase when the moment feels right.

So, how do we ask about price in a way that comes closer to capturing real willingness to pay and not theoretical guesses?

This is where Van Westendorp and Gabor-Granger come in. These techniques guide respondents through a more thoughtful evaluation of price, helping to surface reliable insights that reflect real-world purchasing behaviour. To ensure that your survey yields meaningful results, watch out for the common pitfalls in Figure 6.2 and use tested frameworks to sharpen your approach.

Weak Question	Why It's Problematic	Stronger Alternative
Would you pay $50 for this?	Leaves respondents guessing without meaningful anchors	How likely would you be to buy this if it cost $X? And if it cost $Y? (Gabor-Granger)
Do you think this price is fair?	Too vague . . . what does 'fair' mean?	At what price would this start to feel too expensive? (Van Westendorp)
How much would you pay for this?	Customers struggle to self-report their willingness to pay	At what price would this feel like a great value for the money? (Van Westendorp)
Would you buy this if we offered a 10% discount?	This anchors them to expect discounts	When considering a purchase like this, how important is a discount?

Figure 6.2 Pricing Survey pitfalls.

Use Van Westendorp to Find the Acceptable Range

The Van Westendorp Price Sensitivity Meter, first introduced by economist Peter H. van Westendorp, is one of the most widely used techniques in pricing research.[3]

How it Works

Rather than putting respondents on the spot with a single question about willingness to pay, the Van Westendorp method breaks down perceptions of value by asking a series of four structured questions to identify an acceptable price range:

- 'At what price would you consider this to be great value for the money?'
- 'At what price would this be getting expensive but you might still consider it?'
- 'At what price would this be so expensive that you wouldn't consider purchasing it?'
- 'At what price would you consider this to be so cheap that you'd question its quality?'

You might recognize the first two from the Pricing Interview in the last chapter. In a survey, we use the full set to paint a more complete picture.

These questions work because they mirror how people naturally assess prices. Instead of reacting to a number you give them, respondents define their own range, which gives you a more accurate, unbiased sense of how they view your pricing.

The result? You can identify price sensitivity, understand the acceptable range, and spot warning signs early.

Use Case

Use the Van Westendorp method if you don't know how much to charge or are in the early stages of making pricing decisions. It's especially useful when launching a new product or service and you need to understand what the market perceives as too cheap, too expensive or just right. This method helps establish an acceptable price range based on perceived value, giving you a data-informed starting point before testing specific price points.

Example

If Pour & Prosper Coffee Co. used Van Westendorp to test willingness to pay for their new premium product, the average responses from target customers may be:

- Too cheap: $22
- A great deal: $30
- Getting expensive: $39
- Too expensive: $45

By plotting the distribution of all four responses, we can identify the optimum price point, or the point at which the largest number of people perceive the price as fair value. This is where the 'getting expensive' and 'good deal' curves intersect. For their premium coffee, this is $34.

We can also find the acceptable price range of their coffee at $26–39. At the low end, this is where it's going to start to feel too cheap and may raise doubts about quality. While some respondents may have said prices below $26 were too cheap, $26 represents the Point of Marginal Cheapness where concerns about quality begin to outweigh the appeal of a bargain. The high end of the range is the point where it becomes too expensive to consider, risking more restricted sales volumes. If we had just asked 'How much would you pay?', the answers might have ranged from $5 to $60, leaving us with no clear decision-making guidance and a very wide, unhelpful spread of responses.

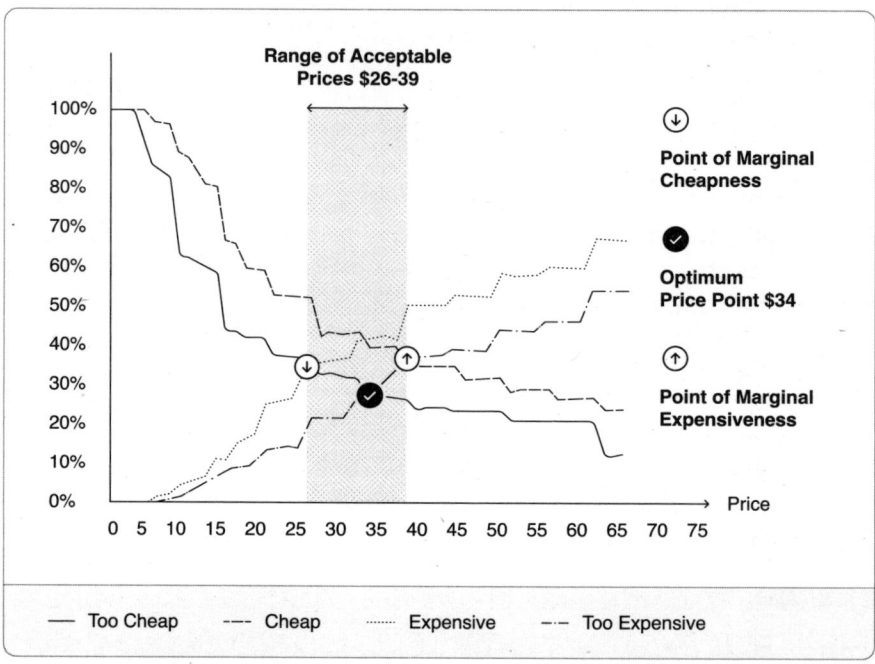

Figure 6.3 Example of Van Westendorp price sensitivity results.

Use Gabor-Granger to Pinpoint the Optimal Price

Gabor-Granger was introduced by economists André Gabor and Clive W. J. Granger.[4] Where Van Westendorp helps define a broadly acceptable price range, Gabor-Granger helps pinpoint the exact price point that maximizes revenue. Think of it this way. Van Westendorp tells you the boundaries – how cheap is 'too cheap', and how expensive is 'too expensive'. Gabor-Granger then zooms in to find the sweet spot, which is the price where you maximize revenue while keeping conversion rates high.

How it Works

Instead of asking for an open-ended price like Van Westendorp, respondents are shown a specific price and asked if they would buy the product at that price.

If they say yes, they're shown a higher price and asked again.

If they say no, they're shown a lower price.

The process continues until a clear pattern emerges, showing the relationship between price and purchase intent.

The Gabor-Granger method provides a structured and quantifiable way to measure price sensitivity and optimize pricing decisions. Here's why it's effective:

- **It directly measures demand at different price points.** Instead of relying on hypothetical willingness to pay, it captures real purchase intent at each price level.
- **It helps identify the revenue-maximizing price.** By analysing the percentage of customers willing to buy at each price, businesses can determine the optimal balance between price and volume.
- **It adapts to the customer's actual behaviour.** By dynamically adjusting prices up or down based on responses, it mimics real-world decision-making, where people evaluate cost against the perceived value in real-time.

Use Case

If you already have a price range in mind and need precision, use Gabor-Granger to help you fine-tune it.

Example

Let's shift to a different scenario at Pour & Prosper Coffee Co. This time, the team is developing a cafetière, a new product in their home brewing line. This product sits in a category where customers already have a sense of what's available and what different quality products typically cost. That makes it an ideal candidate for a Gabor-Granger test. The team can test specific price points and see how each one affects demand and overall revenue potential.

After running the survey, they found:

- $15 → 90% of respondents would buy
- $30 → 76% of respondents would buy
- $50 → 54% of respondents would buy
- $75 → 23% of respondents would buy

If the business priced the new product at $75, they would lose 77% of potential customers, drastically limiting sales volume. On the other hand, if they priced it at $15, they would sell more but potentially leave money on the table by not capitalizing on customers who are willing to pay slightly more.

The optimum price for maximizing total revenue appears to be around $50. The gently rounded peak of the Gabor-Granger curve (see solid line in Figure 6.4) suggests that any price between $40 and $55 would yield a similar revenue outcome. In other words, this product has a reasonably elastic pricing window which gives the team more flexibility to price within this range. By contrast, a sharper, more pronounced peak would signal a narrower optimal price point, requiring more precision to avoid missed revenue.

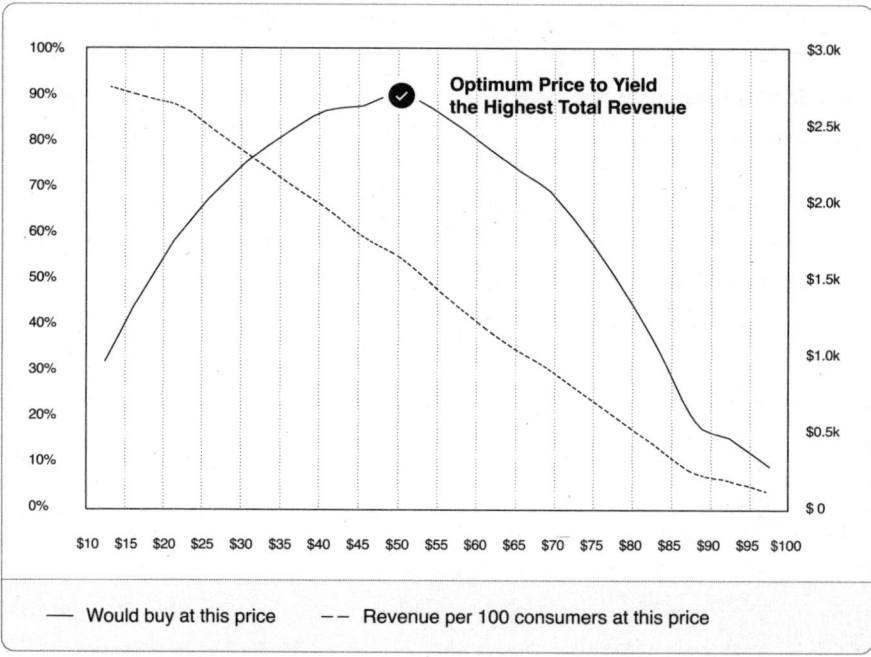

Figure 6.4 Example of Gabor-Granger results.

Use MaxDiff to Understand What Drives Value

By now, you know that understanding how much customers are willing to pay is only part of the puzzle. It is just as important to understand how their perception of value shapes their willingness to pay. If you only ask about price, you risk missing the deeper insights that explain what makes a product worth buying. By uncovering the factors that influence perceived value, you can refine your pricing strategy, highlight the most compelling features, and even adjust your product offering to better match what customers truly care about.

How it Works

Simply asking 'Which features are important to you?' often leads to customers selecting everything. Using MaxDiff forces respondents to make trade-offs, revealing what matters most and least to them when making a purchase decision.[5]

For example, target customers for the new premium coffee might be shown different sets of attributes, such as:

- Rich, full-bodied flavour
- Smooth, low acidity
- Freshly roasted to order
- Single-estate beans
- Microlot beans
- Ethically sourced
- Comes from an award-winning roastery
- Limited release
- Eco-friendly, resealable packaging
- Tells the story of the farm and farmers

In each question, they are shown a subset of these attributes and asked to select the most and least important. This process repeats across different combinations of attributes. The result is a clear ranking of what actually drives customer value.

MaxDiff works because you get actionable insights into customer decision-making. The comparative rating means that customers can't say everything is equally important. This makes it easier to separate key value drivers from basic hygiene factors.

Use Case

You can use the results from MaxDiff to sharpen your understanding of value and make sure you:

- Promote the right benefits or features in sales and marketing materials.
- Optimize options so that each segment gets the value they care about most.
- Align premium pricing to top-value drivers.
- Identify features that might be worth monetizing separately as add-ons or upsells.

Example

We worked with the European gift retailer from Chapter 1 to better understand what drives customer decisions when purchasing their products.

As part of their Pricing Sprint, we ran a MaxDiff analysis to identify which value drivers were most important to the market. The survey asked respondents to prioritize a range of product attributes such as quality, brand, ease of use, and price.

Across multiple segments, two features consistently emerged as the strongest value drivers:

1. High quality
2. Easy to use

Price, while still a factor, was rated significantly lower in importance. This insight enabled the Pricing Sprint team to shift focus in two key ways:

1. Refine product messaging to signal quality and usability over price, particularly on landing pages and in campaign copy.
2. Avoid unnecessary discounting by reinforcing the features that customers care most about, rather than anchoring value to low prices.

The lesson: leading with price was leaving value on the table. By understanding what really mattered to customers, the retailer was able to align its pricing strategy more effectively with the functional drivers of purchase behaviour.

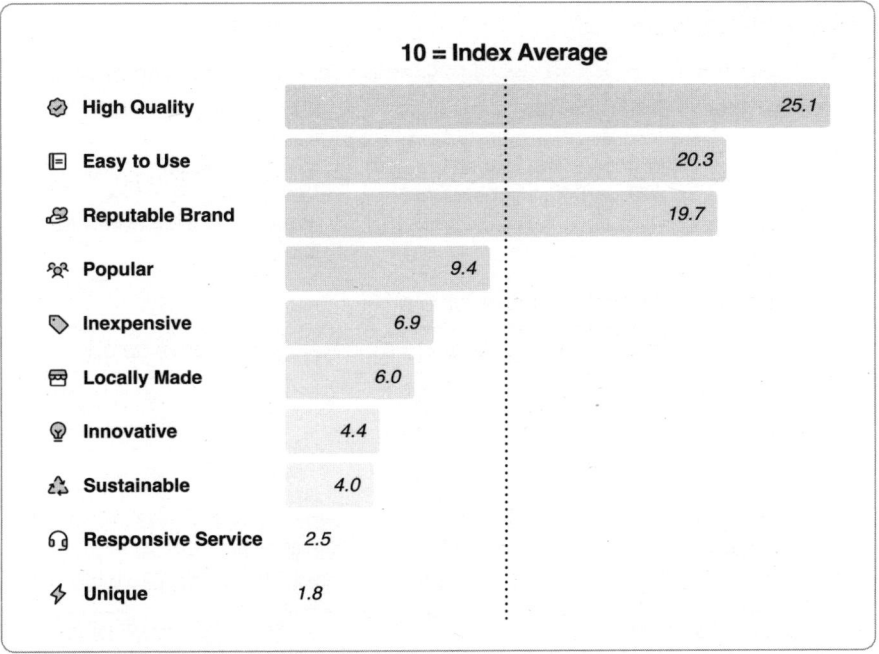

Figure 6.5 Example of MaxDiff results.

Use Other Mixed Methods to Look Beyond the Price Tag

There is a wide range of methods that you can use to dig deeper into how customers perceive value and make decisions, far more than we can cover in detail here. The following table offers a handful of other practical methods to get you started. It's not an exhaustive list, but it should get you on your way to choosing the right tools for the questions you're trying to answer.

What You Need to Learn	Method	Example
Market position	**Brand funnel** A series of questions designed to understand market position and shopping behaviours	Which of these providers, if any: - have you heard of? - have you bought from? - did you buy from last? - are you planning to buy from next?
Value drivers	**Importance rating** A question presenting a set of varied value drivers where users are asked to rank the level of importance	How important would each of these factors be to you when deciding to buy from one provider rather than another?
Trade-offs	**A/B framing** A controlled test comparing different presentation options to understand how framing influences decision-making	Imagine you are buying [product] and see two options, which one would you choose? a) $114.90 with FREE shipping b) $109.95 plus $4.95 shipping
Perceptions of a specific topic	**Likert scale** A question format designed to understand attitudes and preferences by measuring agreement on a scale (e.g. responses ranging from 'agree strongly' to 'disagree strongly')	To what extent do you agree or disagree with the following statements?
Product preferences	**Discrete choice** A method that mimics real-world decision-making by forcing customers to choose between multiple product options, helping to identify the most appealing offer	If you were to buy one of these tomorrow, which one would you be most likely to buy?

Figure 6.6 Other quantitative methods.

Team Review and Bias Check

Before you launch your Pricing Survey, invite your sprint team to review and critique it. The aim of the team review is to answer one key question: will this get us the answers we need?

Sharing with your sprint team can help you catch blind spots, challenge assumptions and stress-test how the survey reads. For example, someone in marketing might pick up on a key value proposition that was missed. Product team members might flag confusing or inaccurate feature descriptions. Sales might pick up on a question that feels out of step with how buyers actually think.

As part of this review, pay close attention to how questions are framed. Subtle wording choices, question order and survey structure can all shape responses. Recognizing and mitigating these biases in advance ensures that your data is as reliable as possible.

Social Desirability Bias

People don't always give answers that are accurate when they want to appear ethical, responsible or generous. For example, when asked how much they would pay for a more ethical product, respondents might overstate their willingness to pay. This is a common issue in pricing surveys, known as social desirability bias. To reduce the risk of this, use indirect questioning. Instead of asking 'Would you pay more for ethically sourced coffee?', ask 'When was the last time you bought ethically sourced coffee?'

Better yet, embed this within a broader set of neutral behaviour-based questions to mask the intent. For example, 'When was the last time you bought instant coffee? A supermarket own-brand? Ethically sourced coffee? A premium roast?' By placing the ethical option among others, respondents are less likely to modify their answer to appear more ethical.

Being aware of potential social desirability biases that may surface and carefully constructing questions can help limit this bias and encourages reflection on actual behaviour rather than aspirational intent.[6] You can then use responses to the Van Westendorp or Gabor-Granger questions to understand different willingness to pay based on purchase patterns.

Question Order Bias

Where in the survey you ask a question can have unexpected consequences. One study in health care found that asking willingness-to-pay questions about three different health care programmes in the same survey led participants to report higher willingness to pay for the first programme, decreasing willingness to pay for the second and third.[7]

Keep this effect in mind when designing your own survey. Think of a survey as an educational journey, where every question builds the respondent's mental picture of your product or service. For example, asking about willingness to pay after a series of questions about product features can make the price feel more justified. Asking about price before establishing value may lead to lower price expectations.

If you're asking willingness-to-pay questions for multiple products or packages, be sure to randomize the order to reduce the likelihood that one particular item is consistently advantaged or disadvantaged by its position. A well-structured survey carefully sequences questions to reduce these effects and ensure that the insights you gather are grounded in real perceptions, not just an effect of the survey design.

Satisficing

A respondent's ability, motivation, and the difficulty of the questions all influence how much effort they put into completing a survey. Of these three, question difficulty is the easiest to control during survey design. If a survey presents too many complex or repetitive questions in a row, respondents may begin to feel overwhelmed. When that happens, they're more likely to take mental shortcuts, choosing answers that are 'good enough' rather than fully accurate. This behaviour, known as satisficing, can reduce the quality of your data and mask genuine customer preferences.[8]

Once you're confident you've reached the right respondents, your next priority is to keep them engaged. Two simple ways to reduce satisficing are to:

- **Keep the survey concise,** aiming for a completion time of 10–15 minutes depending on the context of the survey.
- **Use a mix of different types of questions** to keep the survey engaging, such as ranking exercises, scenarios and the occasional open-ended question. This helps maintain attention and retain higher-quality responses to the end.

By designing surveys with these biases in mind, you can extract more accurate, trustworthy insights that truly reflect how customers think about price and value in real-world decision-making.

Accessibility

If you want your pricing survey to reflect the diversity of your customer base, accessibility and inclusion must be deliberate, not an afterthought. One-size-fits-all approaches risk excluding people whose needs don't align with the default format. Designing for accessibility means thinking critically about who you want to hear from and how best to reach them.

Accessibility and inclusion must be deliberate, not an afterthought.

Start by considering the make-up of your audience. Depending on the demographics of your customer base, you may need to mix survey modes to ensure inclusive participation. For example, CATI (Computer-Assisted Telephone Interviewing) may be more suitable for respondents who are sight-impaired, while online surveys may better support hearing-impaired participants. In some ethnic communities, face-to-face research often yields richer engagement. In B2B settings, CATI not only improves response rates but also signals the importance of the research, while still offering respondents an online alternative if preferred.

If you're working with a panel provider, choose one that actively builds and maintains a representative panel. Use quotas to ensure your sample includes harder-to-reach groups in proportion to your actual or target customer base. This might include segments that typically have lower response rates such as minority ethnic groups, older populations or younger men. Ultimately, inclusive design isn't just about fairness; it's about ensuring your pricing decisions are grounded in evidence that reflects the full spectrum of customer experience.

Plan Your Next Step

Statistically robust data from a well-constructed Pricing Survey cuts through the noise and transforms debates into decisions. Instead of endless discussions about whether a price *feels* right, you'll have clear, quantifiable proof to validate (or challenge) your hypotheses from Chapter 1.

Time and time again, we've seen the moment of enlightenment when a team realizes they no longer have to rely on assumptions. It's a pivotal point as it shifts the conversation from speculation to customer-led, evidence-based decisions. Armed with this data, combined with insights from qualitative interviews, your team will be ready to move forward with confidence. Instead of debating pricing in the abstract, you're preparing to make informed, strategic choices that align with customer expectations, market realities and your business goals.

Knowing what customers are willing to pay is only part of the equation. The next step is to see how these price points perform in the real world. In Chapter 7, we'll explore Pricing Experiments where real-world tests bring your survey insights into a live setting, helping you refine, optimize and, ultimately, set the best price for your business.

PRICING PLAYBOOK: VALIDATE AT SCALE

Follow these six steps to design and run an exceptional Pricing Survey:

1. **Identify what you need to learn**

   Define the specific questions your survey needs to answer to inform your pricing strategy.

2. **Identify who you need to learn it from**

   Pinpoint the customer segments whose behaviours and perceptions will give you the most relevant insights.

3. **Structure your pricing survey**

   Craft clear, intentional questions that gather data on everything from value perception to pricing perception.

4. **Choose your methods**

   Select the right techniques such as Van Westendorp, Gabor-Granger or MaxDiff to uncover what customers value and what they'll pay.

5. **Run a quality check**

   Review your survey as a team to spot leading language, hidden assumptions and unintentional bias.

6. **Use survey insights to evidence your pricing strategy**

   Analyse the results to validate hypotheses, inform decision making and shape your next move.

7
EXPERIMENT WITH PRICE

'You don't truly know your price until you've tested it in the wild. That's where assumptions end and growth can begin.'
RICK MATHER *Former Vice President of Pricing, RS Components*

Through the Pricing Interviews and Pricing Survey, you have gathered valuable insights into customer preferences, perceived value and market dynamics. However, there is one critical limitation of relying solely on what customers *say* . . . it doesn't always align with what they'll *do*.

People are notoriously unreliable at predicting their own behaviour, particularly when it comes to spending money. A price they deem acceptable in a survey might feel too high when making an actual purchase, or surprisingly low once they fully experience the value of what you offer. Doing price experiments in a live test environment helps to close the gap between what people *say* and *do*. They take your research and hypotheses from the realm of theory into the real world, testing how customers actually respond to different price points.

Pricing experiments work as the perfect complement to Pricing Interviews and a Pricing Survey. The quantitative and qualitative research lays the groundwork, offering deep insights into customer needs and perceptions, and the opportunity to gather early reactions to innovative ideas in a sandbox environment. Experiments take this a step further by testing new pricing, positioning, presentation and internal processes in a live environment. Experiments involve less risk than full-scale change and provide actionable data, so you can assess the impact on key business metrics such as revenue, conversion rates and customer retention.

By combining research with experiments, you create a robust, evidence-based approach to pricing that reduces uncertainty and maximizes your ability to adapt and grow. This chapter explores four key types of experiments to bridge the gap between intention and action, each addressing a distinct aspect of pricing:

1. **Price-setting experiments** focus on validating the optimal price point.

2. **Price-promotion experiments** test the effectiveness of offers and discounts to drive specific customer behaviours.

3. **Price-presentation experiments** test refinements in how prices are displayed to influence perception and decision-making without changing the actual price or promotion.

4. **Pricing-process experiments** optimize the internal systems, tools and capabilities that enable efficient and strategic pricing decisions.

Identify Pricing Experiments

When WellSpend Health* began their Pricing Sprint, the team knew they needed to approach their pricing strategically and build a strong evidence base before making changes.

The specific product range they wanted to focus on was operating in a fiercely competitive online market in the United States, selling commodized products directly to customers. While the team understood that their products couldn't command premium pricing, they were shocked to discover they were priced on average 28% lower than competitors. This significant gap had developed over 5 years of unchanged pricing, resulting in a considerable loss of potential revenue. Their mission? To unlock additional revenue within a year, without jeopardizing customer loyalty or their position in the market.

This revenue-unlocking Pricing Sprint included three key work streams: qualitative research, quantitative research and price experimentation. Together, these approaches allowed the team to triangulate insights across a range of data points. The qualitative and quantitative research provided a foundation for understanding customer behaviour and market dynamics, while the pricing experiments offered real-world insights into how customers respond 'in the wild'. But how do we decide which experiments will have the most impact?

After uncovering hidden opportunities in this business's transactional data, the team generated a long list of potential price experiments. The goal was to think expansively, considering every aspect of pricing – from the base price to promotions, presentation and shipping fees. Once the ideas were on the table, we came together for a two-hour workshop to systematically narrow down the experiments based on what was feasible within the company's testing capabilities and the potential impact of each experiment. Gathering the right people in the room created critical alignment across the team and allowed them to make confident, decisive decisions.

---

*The name WellSpend Health is fictional. It allows us to share insights and experiences from a range of projects across different sectors without compromising the confidentiality of any individual client or business. Any similarities in names are purely coincidental and unintended.

Not all experiments made the cut. Attempting to implement all of them would have stretched the team far beyond capacity and diluted their focus. For instance, the survey data revealed significant differences in willingness to pay by state, attributed to varying levels of competition. This initially made testing region-specific pricing an appealing experiment. However, operational constraints and the desire for faster, more scalable results led the team to prioritize a simpler experiment: testing a broad price increase across their US customer base. By focusing on a solution that aligned with both their strategic goals and the feasibility of implementation, the team set themselves up to get faster and more practical results.

The team landed on three discrete trials that would be run as controlled tests on the live website:

1. **Higher prices.** Raise prices to close the gap with competitors and adjust price steps across the range, aiming to boost revenue and margins while maintaining sales and retention.

2. **Free shipping over $100.** Trial free shipping for orders over $100 to determine its impact on boosting Average Order Value (AOV).

3. **Choice simplification.** Test User Experience (UX) changes to streamline the range of options available to customers, reducing decision fatigue and nudging them towards higher-value purchases.

This example underscores how the pricing experiments you choose to run will be unique based on the context of your business. Exactly what and how (or even if!) you test depends on the specific goals you've outlined for your Pricing Sprint and the practical constraints of your business model. For a high-volume, e-commerce business like WellSpend Health online testing was an obvious choice as they could quickly gather statistically significant data. On the other hand, if you're working in a service business with high-effort, low-volume sales, your experiments will be more manual and high-touch.

Remember, experimentation is not limited to changing prices. It can include how prices are presented, how discounting is used, or how pricing is handled operationally behind the scenes. In this chapter, we will explore each type of experiment to help you decide what kind of testing is right for your Pricing Sprint.

Price-Setting Experiments

Price-setting experiments involve testing changes to a price in a live environment to uncover the optimal price point. We'll explore four different types of price-setting experiments:

1. A/B testing
2. Multivariate testing

3. Cohort testing

4. Full-scale testing

A/B Testing

How it works

A/B testing involves presenting different prices (e.g. price A and price B) to distinct groups of customers and analysing their associated behaviours (e.g. buy, don't buy, buy more, buy less) to identify which price delivers the best balance of conversion, retention and revenue.

Groups A and B are randomly assigned and must share similar characteristics to deliver reliable results. For riskier changes, the test group might be smaller (e.g. 10%), while for more moderate adjustments or when faster insights are needed, a larger group (e.g. 50%) might be used.

Use case

A/B testing is best suited for scenarios where you have robust A/B testing capabilities and a high volume of online customers, allowing you to implement price changes subtly without drawing attention. It works particularly well when you can split traffic or customer groups and gather statistically significant results quickly.

Example

A Chief Marketing Officer (CMO) at an online retailer was facing pressure from the board to increase prices. The question: should the company stick to its current £50 starter kits of household goods or increase it to £60? The £10 difference seems modest, but with tens of thousands of customers, it could mean either millions in additional revenue or risk a drop in the volume of new customers. Instead of guessing, the CMO decided to run an A/B test. She worked with her team to split their new customer base into two groups: one saw the original £50 price, while the other encountered the £60 option.

After 2 weeks, they reviewed conversion rates. After 12 weeks, they looked at retention. They found that while the £50 price point generated slightly more purchases, the £60 customers were more likely to make a return purchase within 12 weeks and spent more overall. The CMO realized they'd been underpricing the value of their offering. Based on the new data, along with other indicators she saw from the research done during the Pricing Sprint, the team made plans to roll out the £60 pricing to all new customers.

Multivariate Testing

How it works

Multivariate testing involves simultaneously testing multiple pricing variables – such as price points, discount levels and value-added offers – to understand how different combinations influence customer behaviour. Unlike A/B testing, which evaluates one variable at a time, multivariate testing assesses the interaction of multiple factors to identify the best-performing combination. This approach is more complex but provides deeper insights into how multiple elements work together to drive conversion, retention and revenue.

Use case

Multivariate testing is ideal for businesses with sophisticated data analytics capabilities and a high volume of online traffic, where testing multiple variables simultaneously is feasible. It's particularly effective when you want to optimize individual pricing elements and how they interact, such as the relationship between base price and bundling options or the impact of discounts paired with loyalty incentives.

Example

A head of e-commerce was looking to introduce a new pricing strategy for product bundles. The company sells electronics, and the team wanted to find the perfect balance between base prices, discounts, and value-added promotions such as free shipping or extended warranties.

They designed a multivariate test that evaluated three variables:

- Base prices for the bundles (£200, £220, £240)
- Discount levels (5%, 10%, 15%)
- Value-added offers (none, free shipping, extended warranty)

Over 2 weeks, customers were randomly assigned to see different combinations of these variables. After the test, the team found that bundles priced at £240 with a 10% discount and free shipping performed the best, delivering high conversion rates and the highest overall profit potential.

Based on these insights, the team refined its pricing strategy, implementing the optimal combination across its website. Multivariate testing not only reveals the most effective pricing mix but also highlights how different elements can work together to maximize customer satisfaction and profitability.

Cohort-Based Testing

How it works

Cohort-based testing involves dividing customers into distinct groups based on specific characteristics (such as demographics, purchase history or behavioural traits), and testing different pricing strategies per group. This approach helps businesses gain a deeper understanding of willingness to pay and customer behaviour across various segments.

How you implement cohort-based testing will be different for certain types of businesses. For instance, an e-commerce business might create cohorts based on geographic regions (such as urban vs. rural customers) to test whether location impacts price sensitivity. Similarly, a subscription service could segment customers into cohorts by tenure (such as new subscribers vs. long-term members) to assess how loyalty influences pricing preferences. Meanwhile, a software company may group customers by business size (such as small businesses vs. enterprise clients) to evaluate differences in pricing tolerance and the perceived value of premium features.

By tailoring pricing experiments to these specific cohorts, businesses can uncover nuanced insights, crafting pricing strategies that better align with the unique needs and behaviours of each segment.

Use case

Cohort-based testing is a good fit for businesses with lower transaction volumes and longer sales cycles, where each deal can be uniquely tailored. It can also be used for higher-volume online sales, with cohort-based testing capabilities similar to those needed for A/B tests described earlier.

As you consider cohort-based pricing, make sure your approach to segmenting customers doesn't unintentionally cross any legal lines. In the European Union, it's especially important to avoid pricing that discriminates on the basis of protected characteristics such as gender, ethnicity or nationality. If you're testing different prices by location or using behavioural data, stay in line with GDPR and geo-pricing regulations. When in doubt, seek legal guidance as thoughtful segmentation and customer fairness go hand in hand.

Example

A sales director at a manufacturing company recognized that each deal was high-value, but volumes were low, and the buying process was lengthy. The sales director identified a customer segment he referred to as the 'Rolls-Royce customer' and formed a hypothesis that this group had a higher willingness to pay. To test this, he worked with his team to incrementally adjust proposed prices for each new client within this segment, and carefully monitored close rates, customer reactions and negotiation outcomes.

Initially, the price increases faced little resistance, with clients accepting the proposed rates. However, at a certain threshold, 30% higher than other segments, they begin to encounter notable pushback. Recognizing this as the ceiling for this group, they stopped raising prices, solidifying their understanding of their upper limit and validating the hypothesis that this segment has a higher willingness to pay.

Armed with this data, the sales director established a pricing range for 'Rolls-Royce customers' that maximized revenue while maintaining close rates. The sales team now uses this insight to refine their pricing process for future proposals.

Full-Scale Tests

How it works

Full-scale testing involves rolling out a pricing change across your entire customer base or a significant market segment to measure its impact on a broad scale. This type of experiment carries higher stakes but offers definitive insights into how a pricing change performs in the real world. It requires thorough preparation, including customer communication, internal alignment, and a contingency plan to address any unexpected outcomes.

Use case

Full-scale testing is best suited for businesses with established products, strong customer relationships and a clear understanding of their value proposition. It's particularly effective when smaller-scale tests or other compelling evidence have provided enough confidence to justify broader implementation. Alternatively, it's the best option when other testing methods, such as A/B testing, are not feasible.

Example

Let's return to WellSpend Health, the company that discovered that their products were priced well under other competitors in their primary category. Keen to act and lacking robust A/B testing capabilities, they decided on a full-scale test to implement new prices across their entire product range. The decision was driven by their inability to suppress certain audiences from seeing pricing experiments and a need to capture the suspected headroom on price quickly.

The results exceeded expectations. Despite initial concerns, the majority of customers accepted the higher prices, with sales volume dipping by only 3.7% compared to before the change. Meanwhile, revenue increased by 3.9% and contribution profit grew by 5.8%. Most importantly, customer retention remained stable. The small drop in new conversions was offset by higher-value purchases and no adverse impact on reorders.

This outcome reinforced their North Star Goal: to build long-term relationships and value for customers. Rather than maximizing initial sales at all costs,

Experiment Type	How It Works	Best For	Requirements
A/B Testing	Test two price points (A vs. B) on randomly assigned customer groups	High-volume, digital businesses with robust analytics capabilities	Ability to segment traffic and track conversion/ retention
Multivariate Testing	Test multiple price variables (e.g. base prices, discount, add-ons) simultaneously	E-commerce or digital product teams optimizing complex pricing mixes	Sophisticated testing infrastructure and high traffic
Cohort-Based Testing	Test pricing by customer segment (e.g. geography, tenure)	Businesses with clearly defined customer types	Clear cohort criteria, ability to tailor prices without violating compliance
Full-scale Testing	Roll out pricing changes to all customers or a full market segment	Established products with a strong customer base and a clear price-value fit	Strong internal alignment, change management plan, fallback options

Figure 7.1 Price-setting experiments.

WellSpend Health used pricing to unlock hidden revenue while supporting trust, quality, and loyalty. This example demonstrates how a well-executed full-scale test, tailored to a company's capabilities and goals, can drive significant business impact.

When to Just Do It, Not Test It

Not every pricing change needs an experiment. In some cases, the decision to act is so clear that testing only delays progress. For instance, when prices haven't changed in years, your costs have increased, or you're priced significantly below the market without a clear strategic reason . . . it may be time to move, not measure.

The greater risk is doing nothing and continuing to leave money on the table.

Well-executed price changes rarely break a business. Changes can be tested in live deals, monitored in real time, and even rolled back if needed. The greater risk is doing nothing and continuing to leave money on the table.

Bold pricing moves that are grounded in strong research can actually bring more clarity and alignment than small, discreet tests. They can set a new benchmark, create positive tension, and help your team rally around a more confident, value-led position.

Ultimately, not every pricing lever needs to be tested; some just need to be pulled. Whether you decide to test changes to your base prices or go straight to implementation, the next step to explore is when and how to experiment with price promotions.

Price-Promotion Experiments

Price-promotion experiments involve testing the impact of targeted offers and discounts to drive specific customer behaviours. Think of limited-time discounts, sign-up bonuses and other discounting or promotional mechanisms. As you design a price-promotion experiment, you will identify the behaviours you want to encourage and test different promotional strategies to achieve those outcomes. These could include increased retention, higher average order value (AOV) or faster adoption of premium services.

For many companies we've worked with, experimenting with price promotions has been the key to breaking free from the trap of over-discounting. Blanket offers, though easy to execute, often erode margins and devalue products over time. Instead, experimentation allows businesses to deploy far more targeted promotions that spark specific customer behaviours such as higher retention or increased AOV. By carefully testing promotional mechanics to incentivize specific customer behaviours, companies can maximize revenue while maintaining brand integrity.

We'll introduce price promotion experiments here as a single group of tests. The goal is always the same: to test whether a temporary promotion changes what, when or how much customers buy.

How it works
A price-promotion experiment involves testing different types of price incentives to drive specific customer behaviours. By aligning promotional strategies with business goals, these experiments uncover which approaches most effectively influence customer actions.

Use case
Price-promotion tests work well when businesses want to keep customers for longer, encourage them to spend more, or attract new ones. Rather than relying on blunt, across-the-board discounts, these experiments help uncover strategies that boost perceived value without eroding it.

Example

Because it's the *type* of promotion that varies for price-promotion experiments, we'll share a few examples to illustrate how this plays out in practice. Each one shows how even small internal shifts can lead to more confident, consistent and scalable pricing decisions.

Retention promotion test

The customer retention manager at a meal kit delivery company noticed that many customers cancel their subscriptions after 3 months. To address this, the manager designed an experiment targeting these at-risk subscribers with two offers: one group received a 15% discount on their next 3 months, while another was offered a premium dessert included with each order during the same period.

When the results came in, the value-added incentive outperformed the discount significantly, leading to higher retention rates and improved satisfaction as customers perceive enhanced value from the premium dessert. This insight helped the company design a suite of retention offers that focused on increasing customer satisfaction rather than cutting prices.

Value-add promotion test

The head of a luxury hotel chain was grappling with under-booked midweek stays. To fill these slots without undermining the brand's premium image, they decided to offer loyalty programme members a complimentary spa treatment for midweek bookings purchased at regular rates. This approach drove midweek bookings while boosting customer satisfaction. Encouraged by the positive impact, they extended the strategy to include other value-added experiences, such as exclusive dining offers or guided tours. Their price-promotion experiment effectively increased revenue while boosting the brand's sense of exclusivity and avoiding undermining their premium brand position with deep discounts.

Price-Presentation Experiments

As you saw in Chapter 4, how you present a price can be just as impactful as the number itself. A carefully framed price can nudge customer perceptions, making a product or service feel irresistible, premium or even like a bargain – all without changing the actual amount they're paying. Price-presentation experiments allow businesses to test different ways of showcasing prices to understand what resonates best with their audience, without altering the actual price or promotion.

Whether it's changing the font size and colour used to display the price, testing psychological anchors or experimenting with how value is highlighted, these adjustments are powerful tools for influencing behaviour and boosting conversions. In Chapter 4, we looked at the many different pricing psychology nudges that can be applied to the presentation of pricing. Here, we'll explore two specific types that can be applied to experiments:

1. Pricing page redesign
2. Option suppression

Pricing Page Redesign

How it works
A pricing page redesign applies psychological nudges (see Chapter 4) and design principles to the page where the price is displayed, with the goal of shaping customer perceptions and decisions. Depending on the context of your Pricing Sprint, it can also involve larger changes to the pricing page, such as testing an entirely new Pricing Prototype (see Chapter 3).

Use case
A pricing page redesign is ideal when you want to influence how customers perceive your price and choose between pricing options. This can apply to both online pricing pages on your website or customized proposals. It's particularly effective when you want to guide customers towards higher-value options, simplify complex pricing structures or test new ways of framing value.

Example
The manufacturing sales director you met earlier validated that his 'Rolls-Royce customers' have a higher willingness to pay. Next, he wanted to take the test one step further to explore a second hypothesis: that this customer group is interested in more advanced features and a personalized service than other customer types.

Originally, proposals for these customers included a single offering. To shift client perception and increase upsell opportunities, he worked with his team to redesign the pricing page of the proposal to present three distinct options: a Basic tier that represented the current offering; an Advanced tier with additional functionality; and a Premium tier that included priority support and advanced analytics.

After testing the new proposal, the sales director found that four of the last five 'Rolls-Royce customers' to sign up for the software opted for the high-priced Premium tier, thereby confirming a second hypothesis: 'Rolls-Royce customers' want a more premium offering. What's more, he saw positive signs that these customers would grow into the Advanced tier, therefore establishing a future upsell pathway.

Option Suppression Tests

How it works

An option suppression test identifies the most effective options from a range and reduces that selection to focus attention on options or product variants that deliver the highest value to both customers and the business.

Use case

Option suppression tests are particularly useful in scenarios where customers face secondary choices after selecting a product. For example, choosing from a range of volumes (6, 8, 12, 18, 20, 32, etc.) or colours after committing to a purchase. Reducing the number of options to a more targeted selection can help to minimize cognitive load and simplify the decision-making process.

Example

Let's look at the choice simplification test that WellSpend Health decided to run. They made three specific changes to one of their bestselling supplements:

1. Removed the 4- and 12-tablet options, leaving 8, 16, 24, 32 and 64 tablets available.
2. Set 32 tablets as the default selection.
3. Displayed the main price as 'per tablet' rather than 'per pack'.

The three changes combined option suppression (change 1) and small pricing psychology nudges (changes 2 and 3). Without changing any base prices, these small adjustments increased average basket size and reduced cart abandonment, ultimately boosting revenue performance in the targeted product line by over 18% within just 8 weeks.

Pricing-Process Experiments

Pricing is about the numbers customers see *and* how those numbers are set, communicated and managed inside a company. Pricing-process experiments focus on optimizing the systems, workflows and decision-making tools that teams use to make pricing decisions.

By using the Pricing Process Map from Chapter 2 as a guide, you can identify opportunities to optimize internal workflows. While these experiments are less visible to customers, they can help streamline operations, improve team confidence and keep pricing aligned with broader business goals, even as markets and customer behaviours evolve.

We'll introduce pricing-process experiments here as a single group of tests. The goal is always the same: to test how a specific internal change impacts the way pricing decisions are made or managed. It's the *type* of change that varies.

How it works

Your pricing-process experiments will target internal tools and processes such as price calculators, sales tools or even staff training programmes. The aim is to test small changes that optimize these systems to improve speed, consistency and confidence in pricing decisions.

Use case

Pricing-process experiments are particularly effective in organizations where:

- Your Pricing Process Map has already revealed serious pain points or compelling opportunities.

- Pricing decisions are complex, decentralized, or reliant on large teams.

- You are undergoing strategic pricing changes that are no longer suited to the old way of working, such as expanding the sales team into new markets or adopting an entirely new pricing model.

Examples

The type of change varies for pricing-process experiments, so we'll share a few examples to illustrate how this plays out in practice. Each one shows how even small internal shifts can lead to more confident, consistent and scalable pricing decisions.

Pricing Calculator Improvement

A global distributor of electronic products was grappling with declining gross margins in its US division. Offline sales in the region yielded an average gross margin of just over 20%, far below the company-wide average of approximately 30%.

An evaluation of their internal sales tool uncovered a major flaw. The tool used a colour-coded system to guide sales agents in their pricing decisions, triggering a red alert if the gross margin dropped below 20%. To avoid these red alerts, sales agents negotiated deals slightly above the threshold, closing most at around 21%.

A simple yet powerful adjustment to the sales tool transformed the team's approach. The red-alert threshold was raised to 25%, encouraging sales agents to push harder during negotiations. The results were immediate and significant: healthier revenues and higher *margins*.

Sales Training

A B2B tech company struggled with close rates. Listening to sales calls uncovered a surprising insight: the problem wasn't the pricing itself but the sales team's hesitation in defending it. To test this hypothesis, they designed an experiment. Half the team attended a pricing confidence workshop where they practised explaining the value proposition, handling objections and role-playing tough negotiation scenarios. The other half continued using their existing approach as a control group.

The results were compelling. The trained group saw an 8% jump in close rates and a marked reduction in reliance on discounts, while the control group showed no significant change. The training gave the team the confidence to stick to the price and still win the deal. Armed with this evidence, the company rolled out the training to the entire team, transforming their approach to pricing and negotiation.

Quarterly Pricing Review

A manufacturing company's pricing process was chaotic, driven by instinct rather than structure. To test a more organized approach, they agreed to run quarterly pricing reviews for one year, incorporating competitor analysis, customer feedback and cost updates.

Within two quarters, pricing decisions became faster, internal debates dropped and margins improved by 6%. The success of the test led leadership to adopt the process permanently, turning pricing into a proactive, data-driven function.

Run Pricing Experiments

As a Pricing Sprint team, building a shortlist of experiments you want to run is just the first step. Designing and executing the experiments you've selected may require a carefully choreographed dance between specific experts within your organization or possibly even external consultants. At this stage of your Pricing Sprint, carefully consider who outside of your existing Pricing Sprint team is needed to help you implement these experiments.

Leaning on your Pricing Sprint team can be invaluable here. They can help to identify the necessary internal experts, facilitate introductions and allocate the appropriate time and resources. It's also worth noting that your organization likely already holds a wealth of expertise, and perhaps even some previous tests or learnings you weren't aware of. By involving other internal experts in the process, you'll gain a clearer understanding of what tacit knowledge is already held in the organization as well as the capabilities and limitations, setting the foundation for realistic and impactful experiments.

Whether you're planning statistically robust online tests, high-touch sales experiments or something in between, the internal experts you'll need will depend on the type of tests you're running.

Who to involve for online testing scenarios:

- **Tech** to set up a reliable test environment and implement targeted and measurable testing
- **Data analytics** to measure and interpret results
- **Design** to check that changes align with brand standards
- **CRM** to manage communication channels for promotions or messaging
- **Customer service** to handle questions or feedback during the testing period
- **Fulfilment** to ensure that orders are executed accurately under the test conditions

Who to involve for high-touch sales experiments:

- **Sales** to communicate with customers and carefully document reactions
- **Customer service** to provide support and handle enquiries
- **Delivery** to smoothly execute services or products, especially where tests require a change to current workflows
- **Finance** to forecast, analyse and measure financial impact
- **Tech** to adjust tools or software to aid delivery teams

With internal experts identified, the next step is to bring everyone together to align on goals and prepare for the work ahead. We often run a two-hour Pricing Parameters workshop as part of this process. This focused session integrates new team members into the Pricing Sprint team to support a discrete task, and ensures that everyone understands the objectives, and sets a productive tone for the upcoming experiments.

During the workshop, the team collaborates to:

- **Review plans** for pricing, promotion and price-presentation experiments
- **Leverage existing insights** by reviewing what has been tried, what has worked, and what should be avoided based on past learnings
- **Leverage existing workflows,** learning how past experiments were run and analysed to build on proven tactics while identifying areas for improvement

- **Understand the current state** of systems, including technological limitations and tracking or measurement capabilities
- **Anticipate challenges** in testing, including potential roadblocks such as time constraints, technical gaps or resource availability
- **Set out early hypotheses** and outline potential tests

This workshop creates alignment, sparks ideas and equips the team to run experiments effectively and with confidence.

Get Prepared

While testing pricing in a live environment offers valuable benefits of real-world data, actionable insights and direct customer feedback – it also comes with risks. Being aware of the risk and planning some up-front mitigations can help keep your experiments running smoothly and producing meaningful results.

Here are some of the common risks and practical mitigations:

Risk	Mitigation
Can you support the experiment? Testing new prices or promotions can create complexities for fulfilment, billing or customer service teams.	Work closely with operational teams so the experiment doesn't disrupt workflows. Simulate scenarios before launching to identify and resolve potential issues.
Can we protect the customer experience? When customers see multiple competing prices or offers, it can lead to confusion or complaints.	Use robust testing tools to check that each customer is consistently exposed to only one pricing variant throughout the experiment.
Can we avoid negative 'press'? Customers noticing pricing differences may share their experiences publicly, leading to unwanted attention on forums or social media.	Start with small, incremental tests to gauge reactions before scaling. Conduct qualitative interviews with customers in advance of bolder tests to anticipate potential concerns and adjust accordingly.
Can we ensure the accuracy of the results? Insufficient test duration or interruption can lead to clouded, inconclusive or misleading findings.	Plan experiments carefully to ensure adequate sample sizes and durations for statistical significance. Avoid making other significant changes around the same time, such as big site updates or large increases in marketing spend.

Figure 7.2 Pricing experimentation risks and mitigations.

While there are risks that come with live pricing experimentation, when you shy away from learning 'in the wild', you lock your business into a static state while the world around you evolves. Costs change, markets shift, and customer perceptions of value are anything but fixed. If your pricing remains untouched, you're likely missing out on growth opportunities. Even worse, you may be signalling to your customers that your offering lacks the confidence or value they expect.

Experimenting with price isn't about taking wild, unfounded risks. It's about crafting deliberate, calculated approaches that transform assumptions into actionable insights. Through price testing, you uncover what customers are truly willing to pay. By experimenting with price promotions and presentation, you shape behaviours and perceptions in ways that elevate your brand. And by refining internal processes, you give your team the tools to execute pricing strategies with precision and consistency.

Plan Your Next Step

Pricing experiments, when paired with qualitative and quantitative research, create a powerful foundation for informed decision-making. They enable you to adapt and thrive in an ever-changing marketplace, ensuring that your pricing reflects both the value you deliver and the ambitions of your business.

In the next chapter, we'll show you how to take these insights one step further and integrate the lessons from price experiments, data analysis, qualitative research and quantitative surveys into a cohesive strategy. By combining these learnings, you'll turn pricing into your greatest growth asset, unlocking new opportunities for innovation, revenue and customer loyalty.

PRICING PLAYBOOK: EXPERIMENT WITH PRICE

Here are eight ways to test how customers react to pricing changes in real time:

1. **Live A/B tests**
   Test two price points with different customer groups and compare conversion, retention or revenue.

2. **Multivariate tests**
   Experiment with multiple pricing variables – like price, discounts and add-ons – to find the best-performing combination.

3. **Cohort-based tests**
   Segment customers by traits or behaviours and tailor pricing experiments to reveal differences in willingness to pay.

4. **Full-scale tests**
   Apply a pricing change across your full customer base or market to validate impact when testing isn't feasible.

5. **Price-promotion experiments**
   Test targeted offers or incentives to encourage behaviours like retention, upgrades or higher order values.

6. **Pricing page redesign**
   Use design and pricing psychology to test different ways of showcasing products, services and prices to understand what drives conversion.

7. **Option suppression**
   Reduce choice to simplify decisions and steer customers towards higher-value options.

8. **Pricing process experiments**
   Test improvements to internal tools and workflows to shape how pricing gets done.

8

SET YOUR PRICING STRATEGY

'Before, there was always a nervousness: what if we get it wrong? Now, we have a clear pricing strategy, and for the first time, the confidence to implement it. That's what's been missing, and it's incredibly empowering.'

STUART PEAK *CEO, HeliosX*

Let's return to Pour & Prosper Coffee Co. At the start of their Pricing Sprint, the team found themselves pulling in different directions. The CFO was pushing for premium pricing to protect profit margins and reinforce the brand's upscale positioning. The sales veteran championed competitive undercutting, convinced that lower prices would speed up deal closures and boost sales volumes. Meanwhile, marketing made their case for segmentation, believing a more tailored approach based on customer willingness to pay would yield the best results. Three voices. Three perspectives. Each rooted in logic, yet seemingly at odds.

Early on, the team transformed these convictions into testable hypotheses. Then, they set out to gather evidence by analysing internal data, interviewing customers, surveying the market and conducting price experiments. Each step added a new piece to the puzzle, providing clarity on how pricing could drive the outcomes they were aiming for.

Now it's time to make sense of it all, both for Pour & Prosper and for your own Pricing Sprint. In this chapter, you'll learn how to triangulate different types of evidence, weigh strategic options and make the trade-offs that matter most. Your goal is to set an actionable pricing strategy that aligns with customer behaviour, commercial goals and how you want your brand to be perceived in the market.

This is where pricing decisions stop being guesses and start becoming deliberate, evidence-driven growth strategies.

Prove or Disprove Hypotheses

In each step of the Pricing Sprint, you've been gathering data and turning it into insights. This is all part of building the evidence to underpin your pricing decisions. Just like a lawyer methodically builds the evidence to support their case, collecting evidence is only part of the job. The real challenge is uncovering what that evidence tells you and delivering a verdict. Which assumptions hold up? Which don't? And what does that tell you about the future of your pricing strategy?

Start by revisiting the hypotheses your team surfaced at the start of the Pricing Sprint and matching each to the data you've collected. This will focus your attention on the evidence that matters most and allow you to see how the data you've collected stacks up against each hypothesis. As you work through them, keep in mind that a single data source rarely tells the whole story. To build a robust picture of what's going on, you will need to triangulate. The process of triangulation involves bringing together different data streams such as quantitative results, qualitative feedback, market trends, internal metrics and price experiment outcomes.*

As you bring together data from different sources, you can begin to evaluate which hypotheses hold up and which ones fall short. Most likely, the insights you gather will reveal that some are easily validated, some are easily disproven and others yield contradictory results. Each of these findings help you refine assumptions, avoid missteps and move closer to a strategy that is resilient and evidence-based.

Triangulate Together

The process of triangulation is great to do together with your Sprint Team. Collaborative sensemaking is a powerful way to extract deeper insights from

Collaborative sensemaking is a powerful way to extract deeper insights.

data, challenge assumptions and align perspectives. When team members from different functions come together to interpret the evidence, it reduces the risk of individual biases shaping the outcome. Here's how you could run a triangulation workshop with your Sprint Team:

---

*The book *This is Service Design Doing*[1] is a great reference for learning more about methods, data and researcher triangulation in design research.

1. **Set expectations for a hyper-focus on the evidence gathered.**
   'Today, we're not looking to solve anything. We are just looking for evidence to prove or disprove our initial hypothesis.'

2. **Review evidence related to each hypothesis, and consider one by one.**
   'Let's start with the first one. What did we learn?'

   a. Give each team member a pack of sticky notes and a few minutes to think and write silently, using one sticky note per piece of evidence.

   b. Encourage everyone to note the source for each insight (e.g. survey, user interview, etc.).

   c. Then ask everyone to post their sticky notes to a whiteboard under the hypothesis.

   d. Repeat for each one that you set out to test.

3. **After all the evidence has surfaced, open a short, time-boxed discussion about each hypothesis.**

   a. Invite different perspectives into the conversation where there are dissenting opinions, and encourage a hyper-focus on the supporting evidence by asking 'What other evidence do we have to help answer this?'

   b. Conduct a team vote indicating each one as either proven, disproven or mixed.

   c. Where a hypothesis is disproven, rewrite it to make it true based on what the new evidence has revealed. For example, 'customers prefer annual contracts' might become 'customers prefer the flexibility of monthly payments'.

   d. Where data points appear mixed or even contradictory, it can be a signal of underlying differences between customer segments or use cases. You don't need to resolve every conflict now. Instead, flag them for further exploration and refer to the 'Segment Your Strategy' section later in this chapter for guidance on what to do when the evidence pulls you in more than one direction.

By the end of this activity, you will have a list of validated hypotheses and a collective understanding of the evidence that will soon inform your pricing strategy. Remember, you're not here to guess. You're here to make pricing decisions that are deliberate, grounded and built to grow with your business.

You're here to make pricing decisions that are deliberate, grounded and built to grow with your business.

Let's see what this looks like in practice.

WellSpend Health set out to test a set of core hypotheses. In addition to running experiments, we conducted a market survey and interviewed existing customers.

One of the assumptions to validate was that 'price is the deciding factor when customers choose which online provider to buy from'. A simple statement but one that had significant ramifications for their pricing strategy.

If price was genuinely the most important factor for customers, then a low-cost, high-volume pricing strategy would be a logical approach, resulting in competing aggressively on price to capture as many customers as possible. *If not*, then focusing purely on price could be a costly mistake, leading to eroded margins and weaker brand differentiation.

Here's what they found.

Original hypothesis

Price is the deciding factor when customers choose which online provider to buy from.

Evidence

- Price was ranked 8th among purchase considerations made when choosing one provider over another, while trust, service quality and delivery speed ranked higher *(Pricing Survey)*.

- Customers who switched providers most often cited poor service, not cost, as the primary reason *(Pricing Interviews)*.

- Compared to its main competitors, this company had high levels of brand awareness in the market and was already frequently winning business away from other providers, despite not being the lowest-priced option *(Pricing Survey)*.

- Existing customers had high levels of satisfaction and loyalty, demonstrated by a low churn rate, high NPS scores and positive customer feedback *(internal data, Pricing Interviews)*.

Status
✕ *Disproven*

Validated insight
Service quality and trust play a more significant role than price in provider selection.

Strategic implication

With the hypothesis disproven, they gained the confidence to double down on their position as a trusted health care brand rather than competing as a low-cost provider.

Since trust and service quality were proven to be the primary decision drivers among customers, the pricing strategy shifted to reinforce a more premium positioning. Instead of undercutting competitors, the company raised prices to match or exceed selected competitors, strategically signalling quality, reliability and expertise.

The new strategy also informed changes beyond pricing. Marketing and brand teams refined their messaging to reinforce the value customers cared most about. Language across campaigns, landing pages, product pages and sales materials was updated to reflect this positioning.

The result? The shift to a more premium positioning drove meaningful revenue and margin growth. By aligning pricing with what customers truly valued, the company unlocked stronger financial performance without compromising brand integrity.

Revisit North Star Goal

How did WellSpend Health know they'd found the right pricing strategy? The decision to raise prices and update value messaging wasn't made in isolation; it was guided by the range of evidence they had gathered and anchored in their strategic goals.

They weren't just aiming for short-term customer acquisition, which had previously been a key strategy used to establish a foothold in the market in their early growth phase. They recognized how the approach that got them here wouldn't get them where they needed to go next, and relying solely on acquisition was no longer enough. To reach their next stage of growth, they needed to shift to a more premium price position, and this meant changing their North Star to prioritize retention and customer Lifetime Value (LTV).

By stepping back and aligning pricing decisions with these wider business goals, their evidence-led strategy became clear: a value-driven approach, rather than competing primarily on price, would better support long-term customer relationships and revenue growth.

This is why you need to be crystal clear on what your North Star is as you continue to refine your own pricing strategy. Are you looking to increase profit, drive higher retention, expand market share or shift customer behaviour? Pricing is one of the most powerful levers at your disposal, but it works best when used with intention.

Pricing can help you scale quickly, protect cash flow, improve margins or increase valuation. It can help you win market share, grow customer LTV or encourage specific behaviours. However, as discussed in Chapter 1, trying to achieve all these outcomes at once is not only a dilution of strategy. In many cases, it's impossible.

For example, if you're aiming to maximize profit by raising prices but also want to rapidly grow your customer base, the tension between those two goals will pull your strategy in opposite directions. One move attracts volume; the other restricts it. Without a clear priority, you risk falling short on both fronts.

This is a good moment to pause and revisit the North Star Goal you set back in Chapter 1. Reground the Pricing Sprint team in what you are really trying to achieve. That focus is what will help you turn your insights into action and help you to make confident, clear and evidence-based decisions as you set your pricing strategy.

Align on Terminology

When it comes to pricing, people often use terms like 'pricing model', 'pricing strategy' and 'price' interchangeably, but they're not all the same. Instead, we break pricing decisions into three distinct layers:

- **Pricing model = how you charge**

  This may be as a subscription, one-off fee, usage based fee or licensing arrangement.

- **Price-setting approach = how much you charge**

  This includes specific methods for setting prices such as competitive pricing, cost-plus or value-based pricing.

- **Pricing strategy = why you charge that way**

  This is the overarching plan that connects your pricing model and price-setting approach to your business goals, positioning and customer value.

In the sections that follow, we'll look at each of these layers in turn, starting with your pricing model.

Set Your Pricing Model

Your pricing model defines how customers pay for what you offer. It's one part billing logic, shaping how and when revenue flows into your business; another part value signal, setting expectations for how your product or service is used and what it's worth.

Figures 8.1 explores different types of pricing models and shows how each one supports a different kind of customer relationship and revenue pattern.

This isn't an exhaustive list. Different industries often create pricing models tailored to their specific context, constraints or customer behaviours. Many businesses also use a hybrid model that blends multiple approaches. Choosing the right model creates alignment between billing and value logic. When the mechanics of payment match the way customers experience value, you get stronger retention, more predictable revenue and clearer pricing expectations.

Take Garmin, for example. Buying a smartwatch is a *one-off* purchase. It's simple, transactional and ownership-driven. Garmin also offers *subscription* services that unlock advanced features and network connections. These add recurring revenue for the business and ongoing value for the customer,

Pricing Model	Description	Why Use It?
One-off	Charge once for a defined product or service.	Simple, clear and easy to explain. Works well for standalone offers.
Fixed fee	Set price agreed upfront for a defined scope or outcome.	Predictable for both sides. Builds trust and makes budgeting easier.
Subscription	Ongoing payments (e.g. monthly, annually).	Creates recurring revenue and builds customer habits.
Usage-based	Charge based on how much the service is used (e.g. data, time, materials).	Revenue scales with customer activity. Works well for variable usage.
Leasing or Licensing	Charge for the right to use your product or service usually over a set period.	Protects IP while generating revenue.
Performance	Fees tied to achieving specific results or outcomes.	Aligns incentives. Builds trust and lowers risk for the buyer.
Retainer	Regular, recurring fee for ongoing access or availability.	Creates steady cash flow. Builds long-term relationships.
Tiered	Products or packages at distinct price points in a clear price hierarchy (good-better-best).	Lets customers self-select based on needs and budget. Encourages upgrades.
Freemium	Free entry point with optional paid-for upgrades.	Enables rapid user growth by removing price as a barrier to entry. Monetization comes from customers who choose to pay for added value.

Figure 8.1 Pricing models.

encouraging long-term engagement. The two models work together to anchor the purchase on a piece of trusted hardware, the other supports ongoing use.

To guide your decision, use the five questions outlined in Figure 8.2. In doing so, you'll be able to assess your options with clarity and set a model that aligns with both how your business works and how your customers buy.

If the answer is . . .	Then consider . . .
1. How do your customers experience value?	
Instantly	One-off fee to keep pricing fair, simple and clear
Over time	Subscription model to reflect the ongoing nature of the value
In bursts or irregularly	Usage-based model that aligns with variable use
After delivery	Performance-based model that builds trust and customer reduces risk
2. What level of predictability is needed?	
High predictability	Fixed fee that is stable and easy to budget for
Medium predictability	Usage-based model offering flexibility and scalability
Low predictability	Performance-based on hybrid plans that adapt to changing needs
3. What should your pricing signal about your brand?	
Premium, confident	Flat fees, retainers or performance-based models
Accessible	Freemium with low-friction entry points into tiered options
Transparent and fair	Any model that is simple and easy-to-explain
4. Where do you incur effort or cost to deliver?	
Ongoing	Subscription, licensing or retainer models to support recurring revenue and delivery
It varies with usage	Usage-based pricing that flexes with demand
Upfront or during a fixed delivery window	One-off or fixed fee models that align revenue with effort
5. Do you need natural upsell paths?	
Yes	Tiered pricing, freemium or usage-based pricing to convey expansion routes
No	Flat fee or one-off pricing that is straightforward and stable

Figure 8.2 Pricing model scenarios.

Set Your Prices

Now let's focus on price-setting. How do we determine the specific price point for your product(s) or service(s)?

When thinking about setting specific price points, there are three key areas of consideration:

1. **Approach.** What *method* could we choose?
2. **Implications.** What would it mean for us in *practice*?
3. **Validation.** How would we know it's right based on the *evidence* we have?

Figures 8.3 and 8.4 provide tailored examples of how different price-setting approaches may manifest in product businesses and service businesses. They illustrate the *implications* of what each approach could look like in practice and how you might *validate* it using the evidence gathered during your Pricing Sprint. Use the table that best fits your business model or draw from both if you operate a hybrid model.

After reviewing the tables, we recommend creating your own shortlist of the top approaches you're considering. Map out what each might look like in practice and how confident you are in backing it with the evidence you've collected.

Then, evaluate the options with your Sprint Team. Based on the evidence you've gathered, which approach is most aligned with your goals, your customers and your market positioning? Surface different viewpoints, spot where there's agreement (or tension), then use this to challenge assumptions and build clarity on the direction you'll take forward.

Keep in mind that these price-setting approaches aren't mutually exclusive, so you don't need to pick just one. In practice, many businesses adopt a hybrid that blends elements from two or more approaches to suit different types of products, services or industries. For example, you might use *value-based* pricing for strategic, high-impact offers, while relying on a *cost-plus* approach for simpler or commoditized services. A *competitive* pricing lens may be essential in categories where prospects compare providers side by side, while *performance-based* pricing might suit partnerships where shared risk and outcomes are a strong fit.

Hybrid approaches work especially well when your business spans multiple customer segments, product or service types, or levels of complexity. They also offer a practical way to test new pricing models without a full-scale overhaul. For instance, a retainer might incorporate *performance-based* bonuses, while a fixed-price project could begin with a *cost-plus* discovery phase before transitioning to a *value-based* delivery fee.

Price-Setting for Product Businesses		
Approach What is it?	**Implications** What does it mean in practice?	**Validation** What evidence do we have?
Competitive pricing Set your price by benchmarking against key competitors.	We track similar products across key competitors and position our prices X% above or below, or in line with them, depending on our strategic positioning.	Customers shop around and price-check before buying. Price is a top driver in purchase decisions.
Value-based pricing Set prices according to perceived benefits, rather than cost.	We add a premium to prices for products with strong emotional, functional or brand-led value.	Customers are willing to pay more for key product attributes such as brand, quality, design or sustainability.
Positioning pricing Use price to signal your brand's market position, such as premium or low-cost.	We set prices deliberately to reinforce how we want to be perceived: higher to signal quality and exclusivity or lower to highlight value and accessibility.	Customers associate our pricing with clear brand cues e.g. 'worth paying more for' or 'best deal in the market'.
Cost + Calculate price by adding a set markup to product costs.	We set our prices based on unit cost plus a consistent profit margin. When our costs change, we adjust prices accordingly.	Customers aren't especially price-sensitive and accept standard markups.
High-low pricing Alternate between high regular prices and deep promotional discounts.	We set prices higher than competitors and then run seasonal or flash discounts to stimulate sales.	Customers respond well to promotions but still purchase at full price in between.
KVI pricing Price-setting differs for Key Value Items (high-visibility products that shape price perception).	We price a small selection of 'hero' products lower than the competition to attract attention while keeping prices (and margins) higher elsewhere.	Customers compare providers for hero items. Price sensitivity is highest for hero items. The hero purchase unlocks additional, non-hero purchases.
Dynamic pricing Adjust prices in real time based on demand, supply or customer profile.	We monitor key variables, such as demand, availability and customer type, to adjust prices in real time and maximize yield.	Demand and conversion vary. Customers tolerate/expect dynamic pricing.

Figure 8.3 Price-setting for product businesses.

Price-Setting for Service Businesses		
Approach What is it?	**Implications** What does it mean in practice?	**Validation** What evidence do we have?
Competitive pricing Set your price by benchmarking against similar service providers.	We benchmark against similar providers and align prices to market rates.	Prospects compare us directly with others. Price is a top factor in purchase decisions.
Cost + Set prices based on estimated internal costs plus a margin.	We calculate pricing based on fixed delivery costs (e.g. staff time, tools), adding a consistent markup.	Clients focus on time spent over value and expect transparency.
Performance-based pay Fees are dependent on client outcomes or agreed-upon success metrics.	We charge partially or entirely based on outcomes achieved, such as savings, revenue or other milestones.	Clients focus on ROI. Clients are open to risk-sharing in return for upside.
Value-based pricing Price according to impact and perceived value, not time or effort.	We price services based on outcomes or strategic importance, not hours worked.	Clients see you as strategic partners, not just a supplier. Clients focus on results.

Figure 8.4 Price-setting for service businesses.

WellSpend Health took a blended approach as they repositioned towards more premium pricing. Quantitative research revealed where customers perceived the greatest value, informing a *value-based* strategy for the products where differentiation was strongest and willingness to pay was the highest. Yet, given the competitive dynamics of their market, abandoning *competitive* pricing entirely wasn't realistic. For products that customers viewed as less differentiated and were more likely to shop around for, the team introduced a competitor price index to track pricing across key rivals, which is reviewed weekly and used to inform pricing decisions. For selected products, the team maintains a deliberate price position 2–5% above key competitors, signalling value while staying within an acceptable range. This balance gave them the confidence to price more boldly where they had clear strengths while remaining credible and competitive in areas where comparison mattered most.

The key to a successful hybrid approach is being specific about which pricing approach applies where and why. This enables you to stay agile and strategic, using pricing to respond to the realities of your business and give customers the confidence to say yes.

Stress-Test Your Prices

Before you finalize your pricing model and price points, take the time to stress-test the decisions you've made. Your goal at this stage is to spot issues that only become visible when your pricing meets real customer experiences.

There are two key checks that will help you validate your proposed pricing before moving on:

1. **Forecast the impact.** Will your pricing hold up commercially across your customer base?

2. **Identify where to flex.** Does the model work equally well across different customers, offers or markets?

Forecast the Impact

Taking the time to forecast the likely impact of the changes for your customers and your business helps you stress-test the logic of your pricing decisions to make sure they are commercially sound before rolling them out.

Start at the customer level to spot unintended extremes and understand who may be disproportionately impacted. To do this, you'll apply the proposed model and price-setting approach to a selection of live accounts or customer profiles and look for risks and edge cases where the logic breaks down. Watch for unintended winners who will end up paying less for the same product or service under the new model.

Likewise, be on the lookout for unintended losers, where a price change means that an equivalent product or service cost increases at an unsustainable rate due to how it's calculated under the new approach. Where forecasts highlight risks of larger price jumps for specific segments, you may even decide to implement the change in stages (e.g. 5% this year, another 3% the next year) in order to make the changes palatable and avoid trying to change too much all at once.

This kind of pressure test can reveal hidden risks that aren't obvious in spreadsheets or strategy slides. Even when a pricing model looks strong in theory, applying it to different scenarios can expose outcomes that undermine its viability. These insights give you the chance to adjust your plan, minimize the risk of undesired churn, and ensure that the price feels fair for buyers and beneficial for the business.

Here's how one supply chain monitoring platform used this approach to catch issues early. During their Pricing Sprint, a new price-setting approach looked highly promising on paper. It aligned with usage, was easier to explain and promised higher margins. However, when tested against a handful of top accounts, the outcomes varied widely.

We uncovered a dramatic range in outcomes from a 17% decrease in pricing for one lower-volume customer to a 42% increase for a high-volume legacy client. While the approach made theoretical sense, these extremes would have risked churn in some accounts and reduced revenue from others.

Instead of pushing forward, we went back to the drawing board. The team adjusted the structure to normalize outcomes across segments, smoothing out the most jarring spikes and creating clearer thresholds that felt more predictable and justifiable. The result was prices that were strategically sound, more defensible and easier for the sales team to communicate.

If your business has a large customer base, high sales volume or lower individual transaction values, you'll also want to build in more robust financial modelling as part of your stress-testing. The aim is to gain clarity on the range of possible outcomes and prepare for them in advance.

Start by modelling broad scenarios. Build a set of good-better-best cases to estimate how your pricing change might impact the core metrics that matter most: revenue, margin, retention and customer acquisition.

Here are some questions to guide your thinking:

- How is the pricing change expected to affect customer acquisition, retention and churn?

- What revenue uplift could we see under best-case, worst-case and most likely scenarios?

- What would happen if adoption is lower or higher than expected?

- As key metrics change, what is our critical threshold for revisiting the pricing decision?

Having a clear financial forecast helps you identify both the early upside and warning signs. By involving your core Pricing Sprint team in reviewing the scenarios, you build shared confidence in what to expect and clarity on how to respond if things don't go to plan.

Identify Where Your Pricing Needs to Flex

Looking at how different types of customers experience your pricing can help you stress-test whether a one-size-fits-all approach works or your model needs to flex to serve different segments more effectively.

When you look back at your hypotheses, did you notice different groups of customers behaving in different ways, placing value on different things or responding differently to your offers? Maybe you found that one group was highly price-sensitive while another prioritized speed, trust or outcomes. Or you may have noticed that certain offers consistently deliver greater impact and have the potential to justify a different pricing approach.

If these tensions are showing up as you are working to set your approach to pricing, don't dismiss it; dig in. Messy or even contradictory data is likely offering your team an important reminder: your customers and offers are not all the same. Needs, priorities and willingness to pay may vary more than you first expected. And that opens the door to a more powerful question: how should your pricing strategy reflect these differences to better serve them?

This is your opportunity to consider whether differentiated pricing could work harder for your business *and* your customers. When done well, taking a tailored approach to pricing enables you to address specific needs, hone your position as a valued provider and even unlock unexpected pockets of growth.

These are the signals that your pricing may need to flex in order to serve each group more effectively:

- **Differences in willingness to pay across segments**
  Are you seeing some customers willing to pay more for certain benefits, such as quality, speed, exclusivity or flexibility, while others prioritize affordability?

- **Differences by markets, industries or regions**
  Are different local market conditions, competition or cultural expectations shaping what customers are prepared to pay?

- **Differences in cost to serve**
  Do certain products, services or customers require more time, resources or complexity to deliver well?

- **Differences in perceived value of offers**
  Are some products or services perceived as having a high impact, while others are viewed as everyday essentials?

- **Differences in trust, reputation or credibility**
  Are there areas where your reputation allows you to confidently charge a premium, and others where you might need to price lower or use introductory offers to build traction?

If you answered yes to any of these questions, your next question should be: 'Does our pricing need to flex to address this?' In both B2B and B2C organizations, your pricing can (and should) flex to fit your context, customers and offer. You don't have to tackle every opportunity at once, nor should this lead to an unnecessarily complex approach. Rather, use this lens to find where pricing could work harder. You may identify opportunities to build nuance into the pricing you're working on now, while other opportunities might warrant their own Pricing Sprint later on.

Where does your pricing need to flex, and where does it need to hold firm?

Set Your Pricing Strategy

While your pricing model defines *how* you charge and your price-setting approach determines *how much* to charge, it's your pricing strategy that brings everything together. A strong pricing strategy connects your pricing model and price point(s) to your value proposition, audience segments, commercial goals and internal capabilities. In short, it's your pricing strategy that unlocks the full power of pricing to:

- Shape customer perception and behaviour
- Support your brand positioning
- Align pricing with your business model and goals
- Guide decision-making across marketing, sales, finance and product
- Know when and how to take future pricing action

In this section, we'll focus on how to craft a pricing strategy that provides a clear path forward for you and your team.

The good news? You're not starting from scratch. Back in Chapter 1, we introduced the Pricing Strategy Blueprint as a simple, one-page framework to help articulate your strategy. Figure 8.5 shows how WellSpend Health's pricing strategy evolved using this approach.

Now it's your turn. Return to your Pricing Strategy Blueprint. On the left-hand side, you've already captured the current state of your pricing strategy. On the right-hand side, you also began outlining where you might pivot, maintain or explore elements of your approach. Your next step is to return to this column and make the update that defines where you're heading. This is where your insights, evidence and hypotheses come together, turning the work you've done throughout the Pricing Sprint into a clear, actionable pricing strategy that your team can stand behind.

Start by making your updates to the first draft on your own. Use the insights and evidence you've gathered during your Pricing Sprint to outline the key shifts you want to make. Then bring the draft to your Pricing Sprint Team. Review the plan together, sense-check your thinking and challenge each other's assumptions. This time together as a team is important to shape your decision-making and ensure that the strategy you're taking forward is one the whole team understands and supports.

	Current	Future
North Star Goal *What are we optimizing pricing for?*	**Acquisition** *We are focused on rapidly gaining market share*	**Retention** *We want to build long-term relationships with customers*
Brand Position *What does our price say about our brand?*	**Low Cost Provider** *We compete primarily on price*	**Trusted Provider** *We compete on trust, value and service*
Pricing Model *How do we charge?*	**Hybrid** *One-off, subscriptions*	**Hybrid** *One-off, subscriptions*
Price Setting *How do we set our prices?*	**Competitive Pricing** *We undercut our main competitors*	**Hybrid** *Value-based pricing for differentiated products; competitive pricing for commodity products*
Price Changes *How & when do we change prices?*	**Reactive** *We respond to external forces (eg. raising costs, competitor action)*	**Proactive** *We conduct a quarterly review of our pricing position*
Discounts *How & when do we discount?*	**Always On** *We offer on-going discounts for new customers*	**Highly Targeted** *We boost re-engagement and loyalty with targeted loyalty incentives*
Pricing Process *How are pricing decisions made & by whom?*	**Unclear** *Disconnected teams make adhoc decisions with no final decision maker*	**Clear** *The VP of Growth owns the pricing decisions and consults with cross-functional leads*
Pricing Measurements *How do we measure performance?*	**Unstructured** *Irregular reporting and low visibility across the team*	**Structured** *Regular reporting and review cadence with clear guardrails*
Pricing Psychology *What behaviours do we nudge?*	**Unconscious Anchoring** *User experience primes customers to make price-led decisions*	**Deliberate Priming** *Make decisions based on trust and value, and commit to longer term purchasing*

Figure 8.5 Example Pricing Strategy Blueprint for WellSpend Health.

Completing your Pricing Strategy Blueprint is a major milestone. You now have a clear, evidence-backed direction for pricing that's tailored to your business, your customers and your market.

Stress-Test Your Strategy

Before you commit to your overarching pricing strategy, take a moment to make sure it holds up in two key areas:

1. **Check price-brand alignment.** Does your pricing strategy tell the same story as your brand?
2. **Confirm the role of discounting.** Does your usage of promotions and discounts strengthen your strategy or silently undermine it?

Check Price-Brand Alignment

Reviewing what your pricing strategy says about your brand helps you stress-test whether the story you're telling is consistent with your desired market positioning.

Price speaks volumes about your brand. Think about Walmart (budget), IKEA (affordable) or Ritz-Carlton (premium). The price point signals the level of quality, type of experience and kind of customer the brand is designed for. In each case, price acts as a shortcut to help answer the question 'Is this brand for me?'

But it works the other way around, too. Your brand also speaks volumes about your price.

Price speaks volumes about your brand.

Brand signals such as tone of voice, colour palette, visual design and service experience subtly shape how customers interpret your price. They help answer the question 'Is the brand worth the price?'

Imagine visiting the Ritz-Carlton website. You arrive expecting a certain vibe: elegance, exclusivity and calm. Instead, you're met with bold banners, flashing deals and a countdown timer for a 'limited-time offer' (that, oddly, resets every time you visit). You came prepared to pay for a premium experience but now you're being primed to look for a bargain. The price hasn't changed, but how you feel about it has.

That's not likely to be an experience you'd have when visiting the Ritz-Carlton website, and for good reason: every brand element is carefully designed to reinforce their premium positioning.

This is a good time to pause and ask 'Are we priming customers to make price-led decisions?' Make sure your pricing, messaging and brand identity are all pointing in the same direction. If that's not happening, now's the time to realign.

Confirm the Role of Discounting

Reviewing how promotions and discounts show up in your pricing strategy helps you stress test whether they support or undermine the story you're telling about your brand.

Promotions and discounts can amplify your brand's story or distort it. For product businesses, promotions can create urgency, shift stock or introduce new lines. But they can just as easily train customers to wait for the next offer, eroding perceived value and undermining the everyday price. The difference lies in intention. A seasonal promotion that aligns with your brand narrative can strengthen loyalty and expand reach. A rolling discount that never really ends can do the opposite.

For service businesses, discounts often feel like the easiest lever to pull during a negotiation or lull in demand. Yet when services are priced down without a clear rationale, it risks devaluing the expertise, outcomes and trust that clients are really paying for. Unlike physical products, services don't go out of stock. The story you tell about what your time, thinking or results are worth is shaped every time you flex on price.

Revisit your blueprint and check what role, if any, promotions and discounts play in your strategy. If you use them, make sure they are deliberate, time-bound and consistent with the value you're trying to signal. If they've crept in as a crutch or a habit, it may be time to reset expectations, both for your team and your customers.

Turn Your Strategy Into an Elevator Pitch

You're in a lift with a board member and they ask 'So, what's our new pricing strategy?' You have 30 seconds. No slides. No time to dig out your blueprint.

What do you say?

One of the simplest and most powerful ways to figure out the answer is to distil your entire strategy into a single sentence.

This is the sentence you would use if asked to explain your pricing approach in a board meeting, in a funding conversation or to a new hire. It helps you move from the detail of pricing decisions to the bigger picture of what you are trying to achieve, why it matters and how your pricing approach supports it.

Use this template to get started:

'We charge [how] for [what], because our customers value [what], and our goal is to [business goal].'

Here are a few examples to guide your thinking:

- *We charge a fixed monthly fee for unlimited access to our platform, because our users value predictability and ongoing support, and our goal is to maximize retention.*

- *We set premium prices for our specialist services, because our clients value outcomes over inputs, and we aim to increase profitability without sacrificing trust.*

- *We use a hybrid pricing model tailored to usage and customer segment, because our audience is diverse, and we want to grow both reach and revenue.*

Once you've drafted your sentence, read it aloud. Share it with your Sprint Team and sense-check it together. If it feels muddled or overly complex, that's a signal to return to your blueprint and refine further. If it feels clear, confident and aligned with the evidence you've gathered, you'll know you've landed on something that your team, and your business, can stand behind.

This is your pricing strategy, made simple. A single sentence that connects how you charge, what your customers value and what success looks like for your business.

Plan Your Next Step

There's no single 'right' answer in pricing, but there is a right approach: one that's deliberate, evidence-backed and creates alignment across your team. That's exactly what you've built. You've moved from instinct to evidence and from one-size-fits-all to nuance. The result is a pricing strategy that's uniquely aligned with your goals. Now it's time to put that strategy into motion.

Whether you're making a subtle tweak to price points or rolling out a bold new pricing model, how you implement change is as critical as the change itself. That's because pricing doesn't sit in a vacuum. It shows up in sales scripts, marketing messages, invoices, onboarding emails, renewal calls and board meetings. It influences customer trust, employee behaviour and brand perception.

In the next chapter, we'll help you turn insight into action. You'll learn how to roll out your pricing changes with confidence, ensure that your team is aligned and prepare for the ripple effects – good and bad – that every pricing decision can bring.

Let's get your strategy off the page and into the world.

PRICING PLAYBOOK: SET YOUR PRICING STRATEGY

Here are seven key steps to follow when setting your pricing strategy:

1. **Prove or disprove your hypotheses**

   Review what that evidence tells you about which assumptions hold up, which don't, and what that means for the decision you need to make.

2. **Revisit your North Star Goals**

   Refocus on the single business outcome your pricing strategy is designed to achieve.

3. **Set your pricing model**

   Decide *how* you will charge, selecting the pricing model that best fits your offer, customers and goals.

4. **Set your prices**

   Decide how much you charge.

5. **Set your pricing strategy**

   Connect how you charge and how much you charge to your value proposition and wider business goals.

6. **Stress-test your prices and strategy**

   Stress-test your pricing logic to make sure it's commercially sound, customer-centred and brand-aligned.

7. **Make your elevator pitch**

   Distil your strategy into a single sentence you'd be confident sharing in a boardroom or team meeting.

Implement

9
PREPARE TO IMPLEMENT

It's Monday morning. The final decision has been made. All those customer insights, prototypes and internal debates have been distilled into a clear, confident direction. Attention turns to what happens next, and questions start to surface. 'When does this go live?' 'What needs to change in our systems?' 'What happens if sales drop?'

The reality is that even the best pricing strategies can fall flat if they aren't implemented well. We've seen it firsthand as strong strategies are undone by weak follow-through. Sometimes, it's a high-profile misstep. More often, it's subtle: small oversights, vague handovers or unclear ownership that quietly erode impact. Perhaps the sales team are left unclear on new guardrails. Or an outdated system overrides the intended pricing logic. Maybe a critical stakeholder was never properly briefed. In this situation, the promised outcomes stall, team confidence falters and the opportunity you fought to create slips through your fingers.

Turning pricing decisions into business results takes more than a sign-off. It demands clear ownership, thoughtful sequencing and cross-functional coordination. That's why the next two chapters are focused squarely on implementation.

In this chapter, we'll outline the key decisions and actions needed to build a robust plan and prepare for a confident launch. But successful implementation isn't just about completing a checklist of tasks; it's about people, too. Your team needs to be aligned on the rationale behind the pricing changes and equipped to communicate them with clarity and confidence. That's why the next chapter focuses on clear, effective communication inside and outside the business.

Align on the Critical Decisions

In Chapter 1, you learned that not all Pricing Sprints look the same. Some are short and focused, while others are larger and more exploratory. How you approach implementation will depend on the type of Pricing Sprint you're undertaking.

If you have been running a short and focused Pricing Sprint, you have likely been working on small, incremental adjustments that are quick to implement and easy to measure. For example, you may be implementing a small adjustment to price or refining the way pricing is presented to customers. The change may be targeted to a specific product, segment or channel with the aim of gathering real-time feedback to inform your next steps. For this type of Pricing Sprint, your focus will be on getting measurable results without requiring significant time or resources.

On the other hand, if your Pricing Sprint has been larger and more exploratory, you may be launching an entirely new pricing strategy or introducing significant changes to your pricing model. For this type of Pricing Sprint, implementation becomes a more substantial change programme, requiring even more deliberate alignment, planning and communication.

Whichever type of Pricing Sprint you are running, this chapter is designed to prepare you to approach the change with confidence, agility and a clear sense of purpose. Not every question may be relevant to your specific context, so feel free to focus on the most critical ones to get started on your implementation plan.

Should We Announce the Change?

Customers are more likely to view a price increase as fair when they hear about it directly from the company, rather than discovering it elsewhere. Communicating changes clearly and proactively helps maintain trust, even when the news isn't welcome.* For some businesses, notification isn't just good practice, it's a legal requirement. But that doesn't mean *every* pricing change warrants a public announcement. In some cases, drawing specific attention to pricing can confuse more than clarify.

Do Announce When . . .

If your pricing change will be felt by customers, either financially or functionally, it's best to say something. Clear communication helps to preserve trust and reduce confusion. Here are some examples:

- The price change affects an automatic, ongoing payment, such as subscriptions or software with usage-based pricing.
  Examples: Subscription-as-a-Service (SaaS) platforms, membership fees

---

*For more on how transparency influences perceptions of fairness, read *Transparency in Pricing and Its Effect on Perceived Price Fairness.*[1]

- You're making pricing changes that customers can't opt out of or avoid.
  Examples: Flat fee increases, forced migrations, pricing tied to usage thresholds.

- You're changing how the offer is structured even if the price stays the same.
  Examples: Restructuring packages, adding or removing features, changing service levels.

- You're introducing new charges or removing previously free services.
  Examples: Delivery fees, support plans, payment processing surcharge.

Don't Announce When . . .

If customers are making one-off purchase decisions or if pricing isn't easily comparable because it's project-based or tailored to each customer, there's no need to make an announcement. Here are some examples:

If your pricing change will be felt by customers, either financially or functionally, it's best to say something.

- The price change applies to one-off purchases rather than recurring or ongoing fees.
  Example: Clothing or gifts, commodities like groceries.

- Prices aren't publicly available and are agreed upon directly with each customer.
  Examples: Custom pricing, negotiated contracts or project-based fees where each customer receives a bespoke quote.

- The price change is part of a previously agreed review or routine adjustment, and related communication will happen behind the scenes.
  Examples: Foreign Exchange (FX)-linked contracts or inflation-based increases such as Consumer Price Index (CPI) adjustments or other indexation mechanisms.

- The price change only affects new customers, not existing ones.
  Examples: A subscription business that honours legacy pricing for existing customers.

You're Legally Required to Announce a Change When . . .

If you are leaning towards not announcing the change, it's good to be doubly sure you are not legally required to notify customers in advance. These obligations usually apply when a price change affects existing agreements or falls within a regulated environment and may vary by jurisdiction. Here are some common examples:

- Customers are on fixed-term contracts and you're proposing a mid-term change.
- Your pricing model is subscription-based or includes recurring payments.
- You operate in a regulated sector (like energy, telecoms or finance).
- Consumer protection law applies to your pricing model.

This list isn't exhaustive, nor is it a replacement for legal advice. Legal obligations vary by region and business type. When in doubt, check the regulations as they relate to your industry or get trusted advice.

Still unsure? Here's a rule of thumb: if a customer will notice the change and can't opt out, they should hear about it from you first. Put yourself in their shoes: if you would want to be told, then they probably do, too.

Jenny spent nearly a decade working in monetization roles at eBay. During that time, she shaped many pricing changes across the European business. While some of these didn't legally require an announcement, the team often chose to communicate them anyway.

From a legal and contractual perspective, eBay could have made many of these changes with limited notice. Most sellers would not have been immediately affected, and the adjustments were part of a broader effort to improve fee fairness and consistency across the platform.

However, we understood that even small pricing changes could quickly spark debate within the eBay seller community. In forums and peer groups, sellers frequently shared updates and reacted to fee changes, sometimes before they had full context. The risk was not legal; it was reputational.

For this reason, we almost always chose to communicate early. Messaging was tailored by seller type, supported by detailed FAQs and reinforced through customer service and account managers. While not every seller welcomed the change, the early and transparent communication helped reduce confusion and maintain trust.

When Should We Announce the Change?

There's no single right moment to launch new pricing, but there is a set of basic considerations you can use to guide your decision. Here are the key factors to consider.

Consider Your Product Roadmap

Changing prices without any visible shift in your product or service may feel unfair to customers. Consider timing your price change alongside a product improvement, a new feature release, or a redesigned customer experience to help customers connect the dots between cost and value.

Calculate the Lead Time

Implementation often takes longer than expected. Take stock of where your team is and what other pressures they're managing beyond the Pricing Sprint. Make a realistic plan for when sales, marketing, and customer support will be adequately prepared for go-live. Consider the time it will take for practical implementation, such as updating contracts, sales tools, websites, CRM systems, reseller systems, or customer communications. Leave time for the behavioural changes needed, too. Gauge how long it will take for your team to be trained and confident in how to talk about the new prices.

Check the Calendar

Both internal and external events should be considered in the timing of a change.

Internally, be conscious of what is happening in the business. If customers are experiencing product outages, delayed deliveries, notably low satisfaction or service backlogs, it's probably not the right time to introduce a pricing change. Even if the change is minor or justified, it risks being seen as out of touch with the customer experience. Instead, consider waiting for things to stabilize. Use this time to resolve the underlying problems, strengthen trust and set a strong foundation for any future pricing changes. Equally, if you're launching a new feature, gaining standout press coverage or celebrating an award win, connecting a change to a major advancement in the product or business can be a great move.

Externally, consider seasonal trends and customers' buying patterns. For many businesses, peak trading periods are not the moment to introduce price changes unless you are confident that demand is strong and inelastic.

In most cases, it's better to adjust pricing ahead of a seasonal spike. This gives you the time to learn in the lull and test the actual impact of the change at lower volumes. When demand increases, the new price is already bedded in, allowing you to maximize revenue.

For service businesses, enterprise sales and those with long-term contracts, pricing changes are likely to follow a rolling cadence. Instead of a one-and-done change, updates may be introduced incrementally, aligned with contract renewals, procurement cycles or key moments in the customer lifecycle. This approach allows more tailored communication and often a smoother transition to new pricing, particularly in high-value or complex client relationships.

At eBay, timing was just as important as messaging. We deliberately avoided introducing fee changes for business sellers during peak trading periods, such as the run-up to Christmas or major promotional events. These were critical moments for sellers, who were focused on sales, fulfilment and delivering great customer experiences to eBay buyers.

Even though price changes were carefully designed and clearly communicated, introducing them during a seasonal high could have felt disruptive or opportunistic. The risk wasn't just about backlash; it was about undermining seller momentum and distracting from their core trading priorities.

By planning pricing changes outside of peak periods, the updates landed with less friction. Sellers had the headspace to understand the changes, and eBay maintained trust by showing that it understood the realities of running a business on the platform.

Don't just ask 'Is the pricing ready?' Ask 'Is the customer ready?' The best timing considers what else your customers are juggling and avoids getting in the way of other considerations.

Give Customers Advanced Notice

Different types of changes and customers need different levels of notice. Here's a general framework to guide the timing:

- **Enterprise or B2B clients on contracts.**
  You'll likely be introducing the pricing change alongside renewal conversations. Start these conversations with enough time – typically up to 90 days before contract end – to align with procurement cycles and allow time for potential negotiations.

- **Subscription customers.**
  Aim for one full billing cycle's notice, say 30 days. Include clear information on what's changing, when and what action (if any) the customer needs to take.

- **Customers making one-off purchases.**
  You typically don't need to announce price changes for retail or single purchases. However, if the change is driven by external factors (such as VAT, tariffs or duty fees), and it's likely to attract attention, consider proactive messaging. Use the moment to prompt urgency and encourage action with messages like 'Prices going up from 1st June. Buy now to secure current rates.'

Evaluate the Market Landscape

External factors can create windows of opportunity or constraints. For example, have competitors shifted their prices? Are regulatory changes (such as tariffs, VAT updates, or duties) affecting customers' price sensitivity?

In some cases, timing your launch with broader changes can normalize the shift, reduce friction or even change how you roll it out altogether.

In 2025, American cycling brands scrambled to figure out how to cover the cost of new tariffs imposed on imported components and products. Specialized, one of the leading US cycling brands, chose to itemize the surcharge separately on the invoices of certain products. At checkout, customers were informed: 'This surcharge is limited to specific items and helps minimize the impact of government-imposed costs on the price of Specialized bikes and equipment.'[2] This move not only preserved transparency but also helped customers attribute the change to a broader market force, rather than seeing it as a profit grab.

How Will We Manage the Market Response?

Every visible pricing decision sends a signal. Whether intentional or not, it may be noticed by competitors, customers, investors and the media. Taking time to anticipate how these groups might interpret your move creates space for proactive planning and helps you stay ahead of any potential reactions. Here are some things to consider:

> **Every visible pricing decision sends a signal, whether intentional or not.**

- **Will competitors follow or undercut?**
  Pricing changes can spark competitive responses. Will your shift prompt others to match your move, reposition themselves or lower prices to retain share? If you anticipate a heavy competitive response, now is the time to get ahead of it. Think through the key competitors to watch, anticipate the most likely responses, and have a plan in place to adapt if the landscape shifts in response to your announcement.

- **How might investors or board members scrutinize the move?**
  Be prepared to explain how the change supports long-term strategy. Whether you're optimizing for margin, signalling value or pursuing volume, anchor your rationale in the evidence you've collected through the Pricing Sprint and the anticipated outcomes.

- **Will the press or public take notice?**
  If you're a well-known brand or operate in a sensitive sector, plan to closely monitor what's being said in the news, on social media, in forums like Reddit, on customer review platforms like Trustpilot, and in industry-specific communities. Early detection and having a solid communications plan in place give you the chance to respond quickly and adjust if needed.

During the discovery phase of one Pricing Sprint with an online retailer, we uncovered that our client was frequently mentioned in Reddit threads and flagged on a popular price-matching website. Their market was highly sensitive to even minor pricing shifts, and scrutiny was almost guaranteed.

Knowing this, the team put plans in place well before launching any public-facing changes. Pricing experiments were carefully structured: only 10% of site visitors saw the test pricing to minimize exposure. Customer service was briefed in advance, armed with a clear response script and prepared to monitor conversations across social channels and forums. Regular reviews were scheduled to assess sentiment and adjust messaging if needed.

As a result, the team stayed in control of the narrative and was able to test pricing and implement longer-term changes in a high-scrutiny environment without triggering backlash or confusion.

How Do We Manage Outliers?

This step is about giving your sales or frontline team the opportunity to run the price change through real customer scenarios before you go live. The goal is to test your logic in practice and make sure your team is equipped to explain the change with confidence.

Similar to the forecasting you did in Chapter 8 to stress-test your approach to price-setting, use your existing data to simulate the impact of the pricing change across your customer base. Use this step as an opportunity to give the frontline team members the time and space to understand the model, rehearse conversations, refine messaging, flag where they might need additional tools or support, and identify how to handle outliers using clear guidance.

1. **Run the numbers.**
   What would they pay under the new model? What would shift in their package, discounting or usage terms? How would their new proposal look on paper?

2. **Sense-check the story.**
   Beyond the maths, what narrative is needed to confidently communicate the changes? Does it make sense from the customer's perspective?

Would it be perceived as fair? We'll look at specific communications more in Chapter 10.

Ultimately, this stress test fosters a shared understanding of the new model and enhances frontline confidence. It turns 'I think this will work' into 'I know what we need to watch out for'.

A word of warning: it's easy to get bogged down in endless debates when trying to account for every conceivable scenario before it's deemed safe to implement. In reality, waiting for every exception to be accounted for can stall progress and kill momentum. Instead, focus on what's good enough to move forward. Implement the core strategy confidently and manage exceptions as they arise.

At eBay, we regularly conducted detailed winner/loser analyses to understand the impact of proposed price changes across the seller base. Using historical data, we modelled what each seller would pay under the new pricing if they continued to list and sell the same volume and mix of inventory. This allowed us to spot where the financial impact to them would be minimal and where it might land hardest. Rather than applying a one-size-fits-all rollout, we used this insight to shape our implementation strategy.

For sellers likely to experience the greatest impact, we developed targeted communications, transitional support and time-limited promotions to ease the shift. This included things like temporary discounts, early access to new tools, or personalized outreach from account managers. These interventions weren't just about softening the financial hit; they sent a clear signal that we understood the realities of running a business on the platform and were invested in seller success.

How Will We Know If Things Don't Go to Plan?

As much as we might wish for one, there's no crystal ball that can perfectly predict the impact of a price change. That's why it's important to forecast the impact (Chapter 8) and then set clear guardrails, or pre-agreed thresholds, for key metrics that signal when to stay the course and when to adapt following a price change. Think of guardrails as your early-warning system, designed to help you respond to the unexpected with intention rather than impulse.

Start by identifying which metrics you'll track most closely. These might include:

- Revenue
- Gross margin

- Sales volumes

- Conversion rate

- Average order value

- Churn or cancellation rate

- Competitor index

- Customer feedback sentiment

- Sales team confidence or objection rate

For each, define what 'normal' looks like, agree on the thresholds that would prompt a closer look, and define your fallback position. For example, 'If sales drop below forecast by more than 5% in the first 21 days after a price change, we will investigate and reconsider our position.' Establishing these guardrails provides an up-front, objective boundary between what defines success or failure.

Then, go one step further: define your mitigation plan in detail. What actions will you consider if results fall outside expectations? Will you adjust the messaging? Will you revisit discount policies for specific segments? Having a mitigation plan helps you stay in control without scrambling for a solution under pressure. This matters, because without clear boundaries in place, short-term pressures can easily derail long-term pricing goals.

A global apparel brand came to us after raising its base prices, aiming to improve margins. But soon after launch, they began offering heavier discounts to boost sales, largely driven by internal discomfort rather than customer resistance. Within weeks, those discounts had wiped out the intended margin gains, and in some cases led to lower realized prices than before. The pricing strategy hadn't failed, but their confidence in it had.

How Will We Transition New and Existing Customers?

Every pricing-related change has two audiences: new customers and existing ones. New customers see what's in front of them and evaluate your current pricing for what it is. Existing customers bring a bit more baggage. They'll often notice what's changed and compare it to what they used to pay.

For your long-term customers, some may even recall long-gone pricing models from your company's earliest days. Think of the long-standing Adobe users who still remember when software like Photoshop was sold as a one-time license purchase, long before subscriptions became the norm. The longer the relationship, the more pricing evolution becomes part of the brand story.

If you are moving customers from something they know to something new, putting thought into designing the experience can help the change to feel fair, considered and value-led.

Here are a few strategies to consider:

- **Grandfather pricing for a fixed period.**
  Allow current customers to stay on their existing plan or rate for a specified period. This eases the transition and acknowledges their loyalty.

- **Offer a 'buy now' incentive.**
  Give customers a compelling reason to make a change or buy early. For example: 'Lock in your current rate for 12 months by upgrading to an annual plan before 30th June.' Or, 'Stock up before prices increase on 30th June.'

- **Link the change to added value.**
  Remind customers about enhancements to the product or service to refocus the conversation on what they're gaining, not just what they're paying.

For one staffing firm, they needed to raise prices for legacy clients who had been on outdated, low-margin contracts. Instead of forcing an immediate switch, they introduced new service enhancements alongside the price change and gave customers 3 months' notice. By framing the price increase in terms of improved value rather than just higher costs, they retained 92% of affected customers and increased revenue.

What Assets Will We Need to Update?

Your pricing doesn't just live in your price list, it's embedded across dozens of assets and customer touchpoints. To avoid confusion, make sure every single one of them reflects the new pricing and tells the same story. This means aligning early with your marketing, communications and product teams to ensure consistency in both price and messaging.

Obvious updates include your website, sales decks and proposals. But don't forget the less-visible places like training materials, onboarding emails, pitch templates, help centre content, distributor kits, reseller portals, FAQs and even your invoices.

If you publish pricing online, agree in advance how and when it will be updated. Will it go live for everyone at once? Or only for new visitors or accounts created after a certain date? Confirm the rollout plan with your development team early to avoid last-minute confusion.

One of the key questions for one online retailer's Pricing Sprint was 'How should we update our price match policy as part of a wider pricing strategy shift?'

As we worked with the team to answer this, we quickly uncovered an unexpected issue: two conflicting versions of the price match policy were live on the site and neither reflected the intended strategy. That raised a red flag. We started reviewing other areas more closely and soon found another inconsistency: a key product was showing the wrong price entirely.

What began as a simple policy review turned into a broader audit of pricing touchpoints across the business. A clear rollout plan and coordinated communication across teams is essential to ensure your strategy shows up consistently wherever customers encounter it. Otherwise, your customers (and your team) are left guessing. We'll dive deeper into *how* to message the change in Chapter 10.

What Changes Should We Make to Our Product Roadmap?

Your Pricing Sprint has given you clarity on what customers value most in your current offer. It may also have revealed something just as important: the value that customers want but you don't yet provide. Perhaps they consistently leaned towards new feature ideas during card sorts, expressed a strong willingness to pay for services outside your current offering, or showed unexpected interest in something you hadn't previously prioritized.

These signals are more than nice-to-know; they are powerful inputs for shaping your roadmap. Whether you offer a product or a service, the Pricing Sprint can guide what you choose to build, enhance, package differently or retire altogether. It can help you reassess how you price, what you're bringing to market next and in what order.

One Software-as-a-Service (SaaS) company discovered that customers placed far greater value on automation features than anticipated. These weren't part of their core offering but presented a clear willingness from customers to pay a premium. Instead of applying a flat price increase, the business used this insight to create a new premium tier, placing automation tools at the forefront. It drove new revenue and helped focus future development on what mattered most to customers.

What Changes Should We Make to Internal Processes?

You've defined the pricing change, and you're nearly ready to roll it out. Now it's time to make sure your internal processes are ready to support it. Return to the Pricing Process Map you created in Chapter 2 and ask 'What needs to be updated to reflect our new pricing direction?'

- Do pricing decisions still follow the right approval flow?
- Are roles and responsibilities still clear across sales, finance and customer success?
- Are the systems – like CRM, billing, contracts and internal comms – set up to support the change?

Making sure your operations can support the change turns a good plan into reality.

At the end of their Pricing Sprint, Global App Testing (GAT) revisited their Pricing Process Map and identified several areas that needed refinement before rollout. As an enterprise platform for global software and UX testing, they had been running early-stage proof-of-concept projects for key prospects. However, GAT lacked clear criteria for converting these opportunities into long-term customer relationships, which was critical under the new pricing model. So, they introduced specific guardrails for when to accept proof-of-concept projects to ensure consistency, clarity and, ultimately, increased profitability. GAT also enhanced their reporting processes to improve visibility across the end-to-end sales cycle and streamlined their change request system to better align with the updated pricing and overall commercial model.

Each of these operational updates reinforced the pricing shift, making implementation smoother and more sustainable.

Plan Your Next Step

Implementation is where your pricing comes to life – in systems, in conversations and in the decisions your team makes every day. However, there's still one critical question you need to address: 'How do we communicate the change?' That's where we're headed next.

In Chapter 10, we'll explore how to craft a confident, value-led narrative around your pricing and prepare your team to deliver it with clarity and confidence.

PRICING PLAYBOOK: PREPARE TO IMPLEMENT

There are nine questions to consider when to crafting your implementation plan:

1. **Should we announce the change?**
   If customers will notice, they should hear it from you first. Proactive communication builds trust and reduces confusion.

2. **When should we announce the change?**
   Choose a time when your product, people and customers are ready. Avoid peak periods and give internal teams time to prepare.

3. **How will we manage the market response?**
   Visible price changes send a signal to everyone watching: competitors, media, customers and investors. Identify who might react and decide how you'll respond.

4. **How do we manage outliers?**
   Stress-test before launch. Use real customer data to find edge cases and build your response plan in advance.

5. **How do we know if things don't go to plan?**
   Set guardrails. Define your thresholds for key metrics and agree what actions you'll take if results go off-track.

6. **How will we transition new and existing customers?**
   Different groups need different approaches. Map out the transition experience and make sure it feels fair and intentional.

7. **What assets will we need to update?**
   Audit everything. Update every place where pricing shows up, from website copy to internal templates.

8. **What changes should we make to our product roadmap?**
   Feed what you've learned into future plans. Use pricing insights to decide what to improve, build or retire.

9. **What changes should we make to internal processes?**
   Make sure your operations are ready. Review your workflows, approvals and systems to make sure they support your new pricing strategy.

10
COMMUNICATE PRICE CHANGES

'Wow. That's a big price jump. Wasn't expecting that! But I get it. We couldn't do what we do without it.'

In just a few seconds, this kind of reaction says a lot. First comes the emotional hit. Then the rational perspective. Both are true, both matter, and both show up in the space of a single conversation.

Even when your strategy is sound, what matters in the moment is how the change *feels* to the customer. This is why your pricing communications carry disproportionate weight in successfully implementing a pricing change. A confident plan can stumble if the message doesn't land. Not because the price is wrong, not because the strategy is wrong, but because the story around it hasn't been told well enough – yet.

Most companies never test how their pricing communications will land before rollout. They plan the price change, approve it and announce it. They don't pause to ask how it might feel or how various customers might react. Testing your pricing message is one of the simplest and most powerful ways to protect the strategy you've worked hard to build.

Testing your pricing message is one of the simplest and most powerful ways to protect the strategy.

This chapter is about how to de-risk your pricing communications. You'll learn how to anticipate customer reactions, align your internal team, craft a clear and confident message, test it with real customers and prepare for rollout.

At the heart of effective price communication are four key principles:

Clarity.
It's unmistakable what's changing, when it's changing and why.

Credibility.
The change is backed by rationale that resonates with your customers, such as improvements, outcomes or added value.

Customer-centricity.

The message is framed in terms of what matters to customers, not what matters to your business.

Confidence.

The tone signals assurance, not apology.

Why you should test price communications

Testing gives you a rare window into how customers will react. Instead of guessing what silence means or only hearing from the most upset, you get early reactions that help you refine your message before it rolls out more widely.

Provenance, a social enterprise that helps consumer brands leverage sustainability claims, came to us with a challenge. Their software had become a critical tool for global consumer goods companies – especially beauty brands – helping them track materials, packaging, carbon footprint and regulatory compliance. Although the value they delivered had grown significantly, their subscription fees hadn't kept pace. Prices had remained unchanged for years. Originally set to support early-stage growth, prices were no longer reflective of the platform's impact or sophistication.

The business needed to raise prices to stay profitable and ensure its long-term survival. With annual contract renewals approaching, the team needed to de-risk the rollout of higher prices and anticipate how customers would react before making the change they had planned.

To find out, we began interviewing senior leaders from key accounts. These were high-value customers who had used the platform for years. The goals were simple: test price change communications, understand how customers really felt and refine the messaging to reinforce value.

During one interview with a sustainability leader from a global beauty brand, her reaction to the proposed price increase was immediate:

> 'Yeah . . . it's like nearly triple the price of what we're paying now. I mean, we would definitely need to assess whether or not we feel like we're getting the value.'

Resistance. Reassessment. The kind of reaction that makes leadership teams question everything.

A pause. Then, after a moment of reflection, she shared:

'Honestly, I think the original price was super cheap. I would have expected it to be more at this level . . . the value is probably still good for this price. It's just that it's such a huge jump.'

The same person, two very different reactions.

The issue wasn't whether the new price was justified – it was. The problem was how the change felt. A large, sudden shift in pricing was bound to cause hesitation, even for those who recognized that the current price was far too low.

With this knowledge, the Pricing Sprint team reworked the price communications to reflect both the emotional and rational reactions that customers were likely to have. The updated messaging linked the new pricing to the outcomes that customers cared most about and clearly showed how the platform had evolved in capability and impact. These adjustments repositioned the change as an investment in continued value, not just a cost increase.

The result? Customers who might have resisted the change instead felt informed and reassured. Their initial reaction was acknowledged, and they were supported in making sense of the changes by reconnecting the new price to the value they already trusted. Over the next 12 months, the successful price change drove a 205% revenue increase from existing customers. By taking the time to de-risk the price change, the company strengthened customer confidence rather than undermining it.

Anticipate Emotional Reactions

As you can see from the reaction to Provenance's experience, customers rarely evaluate price changes through a purely rational, value-for-money lens. As human beings, we tend to evaluate prices and price changes through cognitive responses that are deeply wired into our psychology. One of these is loss aversion,* which leads us to be far more sensitive to losing something we already have, like a current low price, than we are to potential gains, like a better platform.

As Provenance discovered, the way a price change is communicated will influence how the sense of loss is experienced. Framing price changes as an improvement in *value* (rather than a pure price increase) can soften the perceived loss. For example, 'We're continuing to invest in making [product/service] even

---

* In the field of behavioural science, loss aversion, part of Kahneman & Tversky's Prospect Theory,[1] is among the most influential frameworks. It shows how losses loom larger than gains, a finding that has been replicated and was validated across cultures.[2]

better with faster delivery, enhanced features and improved support. Next month, our pricing will be updated to reflect the added value.'

This sensitivity to loss goes hand-in-hand with a sensitivity to fairness. Sudden, unexplained price hikes can feel unfair to customers. The larger the increase, the greater the risk. Similar to loss aversion, customers are more likely to accept a price change if they are given a reason for the change that is linked to factors they perceive as fair, such as better service, rising supplier costs or higher wages for employees.

The scale of the price change shapes how much explanation customers expect. The research you've done so far will tell you how big a planned change will feel to your customers: is it likely that your change will register as large or small? Smaller increases can often be explained briefly. In fact, research suggests that overexplaining small price changes increases cognitive load and risks drawing unfavourable attention. Larger changes, however, require greater transparency and more detail to help customers draw connections between what they're paying and the value they are getting in return.[3]

Anticipating customer reactions is only one piece of the pricing communications puzzle. The same psychological aversions to price changes are likely to surface within your own organization, particularly among the teams responsible for delivering the news. Sales, customer service and account management teams often experience customer frustration firsthand. When they lack confidence in the rationale behind the change or feel that it's unfair, this can seep into their communication and undermine both the message and your customers' trust.

How your teams present the pricing story to the market plays a major role in determining whether or not it resonates with customers. The most effective price changes occur when both customers and internal teams understand what's changing and *why*.

The most effective price changes occur when internal teams understand what's changing and *why*.

When internal teams understand the logic behind the decision and feel confident in its fairness, they are more likely to deliver the message clearly, consistently and with conviction. So, ensure that your pricing story is heard as you intend by involving customer-facing teams in the process of anticipating customer reactions and aligning on key messages.

This is the moment to bring in reinforcements to your Sprint Team, gathering a mix of voices, insights and expertise to shape both the message and the delivery plan.

Bring the Sprint Team and your reinforcements together for a hands-on workshop. This collaborative session sets the stage for what is ahead and draws on your team's past experience and collective expertise. It enables you to anticipate customer reactions and begin to build a clear, confident communications plan.

Step 1: Review Response to Past Price Changes

Start by looking back. Review how customers responded to previous price changes, both the successes and the struggles. What worked well? What didn't land as intended? What lessons can inform this next change?

Wherever possible, bring real artefacts into the session (such as previous price change emails, customer feedback or quotes from customer service transcripts) so the team can work with tangible examples. The goal is to create a shared understanding of the past so the team can apply those insights to shape a better approach this time around.

Step 2: Anticipate Customer Reactions

Next, work through a series of structured scenarios based on different customer segments to explore potential reactions, both desirable and undesirable. Here, you can lean on the scenarios you already began exploring in Chapter 8 as you forecasted the impact of the changes.

Example scenario
You're a long-time customer who has renewed at the same price for years. You've just received notice that new subscribers will be paying a higher rate than you are. Your price will be maintained for the next 12 months, then increase to the higher rate.

Questions to explore with the team:

- What's your first reaction to seeing this?
- What negative thoughts or concerns come to mind?
- What positive signals do you take from this?
- What would you need to see or hear to feel reassured and confident?

The aim is not to predict every complaint. Instead, this exercise helps put the team in the customer's shoes and understand fairness concerns, flag potential objections and identify opportunities to reinforce value. Work through the leading scenarios to anticipate the most likely reactions.

Step 3: Align on a Shared Vision for Success

With the team now grounded in customer perspectives, shift the focus to defining what success looks like for your price communication. Ask the team:

- How do we want the wider team to talk about the price change internally?

- What headlines do we want to be able to share with the board after the price change?

- What would we want to see if this were covered in the media or discussed on social channels?

- What feedback do we hope to hear directly from customers?

This shared vision acts as a guiding light, ensuring that every decision about wording, timing and delivery aligns with the outcomes that the team is working toward.

Step 4: Define Key Principles

Work with the team to capture the essential messages that should appear in every version of the communication, regardless of format or audience. Then, define key principles that shape *how* you'll say it: for example, 'Lead with outcomes' or 'Avoid apologetic language'.

These foundations keep your message consistent, even when tailored to different segments or delivery channels.

Select the Channels for Communicating Your Price Change

Before crafting the message itself, take time to consider *how* your pricing change communication will be delivered. The channel, format, tone and level of personalisation will all influence how the message is received, especially across different customer types. Use Figure 10.1 to help weigh up your options.

Different channels work better for different customers and contexts, so think about how your communication channels can work together. For example, after receiving an email about a price change, a customer may log on to their account to make changes, and both channels should convey the same message. This layered approach ensures that your message is seen, understood and reinforced in all the right places.

Channel	Best For	Strengths	Potential Pitfalls
1:1 call or meeting	Enterprise clients, strategic accounts	Personal, high-trust, allows for two-way dialogue	Time-intensive, quality of delivery will vary by person
Email (personalized)	Mid-sized clients, managed accounts	Scalable, with room for tailoring and explanation	Quality of delivery may vary by sender
Email (automated)	Large customer base, self-serve accounts	Efficient, measurable, can be easily segmented and scheduled in advance	Risk of being ignored or missed
SMS or WhatsApp message	Mobile-first users	High visibility, prompts quick action	Must be concise, may feel intrusive if overused or unexpected
In-app message	Active users and self-serve SaaS customers	Real-time and contextual	May be missed by less frequent users
Landing page / FAQ	Supporting comms for self-serve customers and customer support	Provides a consistent reference point for simple or routine changes	Risk of being missed, so should not be the *only* channel for major or sensitive changes

Figure 10.1 Communication channels.

Craft a Compelling Message

You've anticipated customer reactions, aligned internally, and made deliberate choices about *how* and *where* to deliver the message. Now it's time to craft *what* you'll say.

There are two key steps to set your team up for success.

First, identify a single core asset as your 'communication zero'. This could be an email to customers, an account manager call script or a customer-facing FAQ page. Choose whatever channel and format will be used first or carry the most weight. This will become your anchor message and the version to test, refine and align on before adapting it for other use cases. Once the team agrees on this foundational message, it will be far easier to tailor it for different audiences or delivery channels without reopening core decisions every time.

Secondly, appoint a single person to write the first draft. Writing by committee is rarely effective, as multiple voices pulling in different directions can quickly dilute both clarity and confidence. Instead, nominate someone who understands the strategy and has the writing skills to synthesize the key messages into a clear, cohesive communication.

If the team has capacity, ask two or three people to draft the same core message independently. This can add valuable diversity of thought while still avoiding the pitfalls of group writing. AI tools can also generate multiple variations quickly, offering new angles or phrasing you might not have considered. Once those initial drafts exist, the team can review and select the best elements to combine into the final message. Whether you start with one draft or several, the goal is the same: a unified, confident message that sets the tone for the entire communication process.

Include the Core Elements

While the specific content will vary based on your strategy, most effective price change communications include a core set of elements:

1. **What and when.** Clearly state what is changing and when. Avoid ambiguity, which leads to confusion, which creates unnecessary resistance.

2. **Call to action.** What, if anything, does the customer need to do? Are they required to opt in, opt out or take no action? Make this explicit.

Based on the scale of the change and what different segments of your customers value, you may also want to include:

3. **Further information.** Include a clear path for follow-up, whether it's a support contact, an FAQ page, or a dedicated landing page that explains the change in more detail.

4. **Value reminder.** Reinforce the value that the customer is already receiving, especially if that value has grown over time with no price increases. This could include new features, recent improvements, or proven ROI that reinforces why the product or service is worth the updated price.

5. **Rationale.** Share the reasons behind the price increase, whether it's due to rising supplier costs, higher wages, regulatory changes or investments in improved service. It doesn't need to be long, but it does need to be credible and honest.

6. **Other information.** Consider what else a customer might want to know if they were receiving this communication. For example:

   ○ Are there alternative options available at different price points?

- What support is available?
- Can customers save by paying annually vs. monthly?

These elements won't apply to every situation; however, where appropriate, they provide the context for turning a price change into a conversation about choice, fit and value.

Choose Your Narrative

The way you choose to tell the story will alter how customers respond. Here are five narrative approaches to communicating a price change, some of which you may have encountered in your own inbox from other companies.

The Emotional Story

This approach frames the price change around the broader mission and impact. It works well for purpose-driven businesses or brands looking to spark a sense of being 'in it together'.

'We started this journey together to help you achieve [goal]. To keep delivering the innovation you expect, we're adjusting our pricing to support the next phase of that journey.'

The Business Justification

This is a transparent, facts-first approach, where you explain the economic or operational reasons behind the change. This can work well in B2B contexts where logic and cost structures resonate with customers.

'Over the past 3 years, we've invested heavily in security, performance and new features, but our pricing hasn't kept pace with those investments. To continue supporting your business at the level you expect, our pricing will be updated.'

The Unapologetic Change

This is a simple, factual delivery that does not involve emotional appeals or lengthy explanations. It's often used by businesses with significant market power or in cases where the price change is expected and further justification would undermine the change.

'Starting on [date], the new price for all [type] subscriptions will be [X].'

The Value Difference

This frames the price change as a reflection of tangible improvements in value. It's particularly useful when you've added major features, services or benefits that enhance the product.

> 'We've introduced new tools, expanded support hours and enhanced reporting capabilities – all designed to help you get more value. To reflect these improvements, our pricing will be updated.'

Apple to Pears

In some cases, the most effective way to communicate a price change is to reframe the entire offering. This is especially useful when you're making a bigger change to how your offer is structured, by changing what the customer is buying or how it's packaged. When customers move to a new plan, bundle or pricing structure, it becomes harder to make direct comparisons. This shift helps focus the conversation on value rather than just cost.

Narrative Type	Best For	What It Does	Potential Pitfalls
The Emotional Story	Mission-led brands, loyal customer bases, community-focused offerings	Builds emotional connection, reinforces shared journey	May feel insincere if relationship isn't strong
The Business Justification	B2B clients, procurement-led accounts, cost-sensitive buyers	Frames the change in operational or financial logic	Can come across as impersonal or overly rational
The Unapologetic Change	High market power, expected or routine price changes	Delivers a clear, confident statement without emotional framing	May feel abrupt if used without care or context
The Value Difference	Feature-rich updates, recent product improvements, SaaS and service upgrades	Emphasizes added value, links pricing to new capabilities	Needs real, recent improvements to back up the claim
Apples to Pears	Customers moving to new plans, bundles or pricing models	Reframes the basis of comparison to shift the conversation to value	Can cause confusion if changes aren't clearly explained or mapped

Figure 10.2 Narrative styles for price change communications.

'We're updating how we structure our plans to give you more flexibility and ensure that your pricing better reflects the features you actually use.'

Once you understand the different narrative styles, the next question is: which one fits your context best? Use Figure 10.2 to guide your choice.

Once you've crafted your message and chosen the right narrative, it's time to put it to the test by checking how it lands with real customers before you roll it out at scale.

Test Communications

With your communication zero in hand, it's time to test it with customers through structured interviews. The goal of this step is simple: What works? What doesn't? What should we prepare for?

Testing helps you move beyond assumptions, giving you real feedback on how your message will land in terms of clarity and emotional response. These interviews follow a similar approach to the customer conversations covered in Chapter 5, so refer back to that chapter for guidance on recruiting participants and setting up your sessions.

Sample interview guide

1. **Ask open questions.**
   Put the customer at ease, ask open questions about the value that the product/service brings, and understand different use cases.

2. **Disclose.**
   Set expectations for the discussion: 'We're planning a price change in the near future, and today we'd like to get your reflections, ideas and suggestions about how we communicate it.'

3. **Learn.**
   Ask open questions to understand how they engage with your business and what they remember about the price they pay: 'Tell me about [reference the product/service].'

   - 'What is the [monthly/annual/average] amount you pay?'
     If they don't know, ask: 'If you had to take a guess . . . how much would you expect you are paying?'

- 'What is included in that cost?'
- 'Is there anything you would like to get from [product/service] that you are not getting right now?'

4. Reveal.

Share your screen with the draft of your communication zero. 'Imagine you received this message in your inbox. I'm going to give you a minute to read it, so let me know when you're ready.'

- 'What are your first impressions?'
- 'What questions do you have?'
- 'What do these changes mean for you?'
- 'What is your view of the new price(s)?'
- 'What would you do next?'

5. Reassure.

Close by setting expectations for what's next: 'This change is not final, and your existing price will still apply until you receive official communication from us saying otherwise.'

Compare Reactions from Existing and Prospective Customers

Existing customers are anchored to your current price, so their reactions will naturally differ from prospects who come with no price reference point. If you tested a separate pricing prototype with prospective customers in Chapter 5, comparing sentiment between existing and prospective customers will help you understand how reactions to price are likely to differ. In turn, this allows you to evaluate whether concerns from existing customers are significant enough to warrant a phased rollout (see Chapter 9).

For example, if prospective customers see the new price as fair value for money but existing customers express strong backlash, you might decide to introduce the price change for new customers first while communicating a temporary grace period for existing customers. This approach gives loyal customers time to adjust while maintaining price integrity for new sales.

Your goals here are to learn how others interpret the message, where confusion creeps in and where resistance is likely to surface. Armed with these insights, you can refine the communication, equip your teams to handle objections and increase the odds of a smooth rollout.

Why you shouldn't skip price communications testing

A direct-to-consumer drinks brand was preparing to respond to external cost increases as new VAT rules and changing import regulations meant that their margins were strained. Rather than passing on the full impact to customers, they made a deliberate, customer-friendly decision to absorb a significant portion of the increased costs themselves.

They crafted an email to communicate this to customers, explaining that while some prices would rise, many would stay the same and a few prices would even drop. The message was intended to be transparent, fair and reassuring, yet early feedback revealed it would be confusing to customers, some of whom responded:

'Are you raising prices or lowering them?'
'It sounds like a hedge – what's actually happening?'

More importantly, the core message was buried: that the company was absorbing the majority of the cost increase to protect its customers.

The problem wasn't the decision; it was the delivery. The well-intentioned nuance had muddied the message.

The team revised their approach and led with the big idea: 'We're shielding you from rising costs.' To reinforce this commitment, they introduced a Price Promise, guaranteeing that several bestselling products wouldn't see any further increases for the rest of the year.

This simple but strategic promise offered certainty at a time of external change, and helped customers feel that the company had their back. The message landed far better and customers understood that the brand was taking a hit, not passing one on. The real surprise came later: when the team reviewed the results after 3 months, they found that customers who received the price communication actually had *higher* retention than a control group of those who didn't. A message about price changes had, in the end, strengthened loyalty.

Get Ready to Talk Pricing

Whether they're handling routine renewal conversations or responding to direct objections, your sales, customer success and customer service teams need more than just the headline price change. They need to understand the *why* behind the change, *how* it connects to the business strategy and *what* to communicate in a way that feels credible and customer-centric.

It's time to package up the work you've done so far into a simple kit that can be used by front-line staff to deliver a consistent, confident message while allowing flexibility to respond based on the customer and context.

As you begin to assemble a package for your team, be sure to cover:

- **The basics.** What's changing, when it's happening and which customers are affected. Keep this clear, factual and easy to reference.

- **The rationale.** Why it's happening, grounded in both business realities and customer value. Focus on ensuring that this section communicates credibility, transparency and brand alignment.

- **Objection handling.** Outline the most likely objections and provide clear, adaptable responses. These responses should allow team members to acknowledge concerns, address objections and reinforce value.

- **Next steps.** What customers need to do (if anything). Where possible, make next steps simple and friction-free.

- **Options and alternatives.** Outline any options or alternatives available, particularly for customers most likely to consider leaving. Focus on tools to support retention, such as reviewing whether they're on the right plan, rather than offering deep discounts that could undermine the price change itself.

- **FAQ and talking points.** Include any other common questions that your teams expect to encounter, along with clear, confident responses.

Some customers will accept the change immediately; others will push back. Your team needs to be ready for tough conversations. Equipping them with clear framing and flexible responses will give them the tools they need to respond to common objections.

Even with the best FAQs and talking points, practice matters. Consider running short role-play sessions to help frontline personnel get comfortable using the messaging in real conversations, giving them the confidence to respond calmly and consistently. These sessions should cover a range of realistic customer scenarios, from casual inquiries to high-stakes renewal negotiations. Encourage teams to experiment with different tones and framing techniques so they develop the flexibility to adapt the message to different scenarios.

Plan Your Next Step

You've crafted a confident message, and equipped your team to deliver it with clarity. That's no small feat.

Strong pricing communications strengthen your positioning, deepen customer trust and set the foundation for realizing what you set out to achieve with your pricing change.

Now, as your new pricing goes live, it's time to shift gears from planning to learning.

In Chapter 11, we'll explore how to measure the impact of your pricing decisions, from early signs of customer engagement to long-term gains in revenue, retention and profitability. You'll learn what to monitor, what to expect and how to respond quickly if things don't go as planned.

PRICING PLAYBOOK: COMMUNICATE PRICE CHANGES

Here are seven key steps to follow when preparing to communicate your price changes:

1. **Anticipate reactions**
   Explore how different customers might respond, both positively and negatively.

2. **Align on success**
   Get clear on what success looks like, both internally and externally.

3. **Define key messages**
   Agree on the key talking points and guiding principles for how we say them.

4. **Select the channels**
   Choose the right mix of communication channels for each audience.

5. **Craft the message**
   Design customer-centric messaging that is clear, credible, confident and grounded in the right narrative.

6. **Test before rollout**
   Test messaging with real customers and iterate based on their feedback.

7. **Get ready to talk pricing**
   Make sure the team are briefed, aligned and ready to speak about pricing consistently and confidently.

11
MEASURE THE IMPACT

Imagine you are 10 minutes into a quarterly business review. You've just shared the results of your highly successful price change. The CEO leans back and says, 'I'm not convinced pricing had anything to do with it.' Across the table, the head of marketing adds, 'Let's be honest, the growth came from our new campaign, not from changing the price.'

If you've ever sat in a meeting like this, you'll know how quickly pricing can come under fire. When results start rolling in, there's often a rush to either claim credit or cast doubt. Given pricing rarely operates in a vacuum, it can be tricky to tell what really made the difference. A feature release, a sales push, a new competitor or a fresh marketing campaign could all land at the same time.

It's up to you to show the business that pricing works. Measuring the impact is how you determine the value of all your hard work and capture the win. Without it, even the best pricing decisions can go unnoticed. You risk falling into a blind spot, where progress is either unclear or wrongly attributed to something else.

Measurement doesn't have to be perfect to be powerful, but it does need to be deliberate. Done well, it builds trust across your team, leadership and the wider business. It turns pricing from a tactical lever into a strategic capability that earns investment, attention and influence.

By treating measurement as an integral part of pricing, three things happen:

- You build confidence in the strategy by using real-world evidence rather than instinct or anecdote.
- You spot friction early, giving you the chance to adapt before problems escalate.
- You demonstrate progress to stakeholders who need to see results, not just intentions.

While it may start with looking back, measuring the impact of pricing also helps you plan for the future. It provides you with the evidence and confidence to influence what comes next and equips you with the proof points, patterns and language to shape future pricing decisions.

In this chapter, we'll show you how to cut through the noise and make sense of what's really driving impact. You'll learn how to track results over time, isolate the role pricing played and keep measurement simple enough to stick.

Why measurement matters

In the first days after launch, emotions run high and any silence feels ominous. Teams can swing from 'we've nailed it' to 'what have we done?' in a single conversation. There's often a scramble to make sense of early signals, even when it's too soon to draw conclusions.

This is where measurement gives the team something solid to hold onto while things settle. It also builds a shared view of progress, so no one is stuck guessing what's really going on.

Not every outcome will be immediate or obvious. Some results take weeks or months to surface. Others are hiding in plain sight, if you know where to look. You might notice a lift in customer retention before you see changes in average spend. You might observe stronger uptake in one segment and hesitation in another. Sales conversations might feel easier. Pushback might drop.

These are all signals to capture, interpret and act on. Without a deliberate approach to measurement, subtle shifts are easily missed and valuable insights slip through the cracks.

When we started working with a consumer brand in the United States, they'd previously launched new pricing with care and discipline. However, one crucial piece was missing. They hadn't agreed on how they would measure success. There was no shared view of which metrics to track, what timeframe to assess or how to separate the impact of pricing from other business activities.

As a result, the impact of the price changes was still being debated almost a year later. Sales were up, though no one could say whether pricing had made the difference. Conversion rates had shifted, though there was no agreement on which segments had improved or declined. Without a clear baseline or measurement plan, the team could not tell.

What could have been a celebrated success and compelling proof for the power of pricing became another source of internal friction. Pricing conversations stalled and confidence dropped as no one felt clear on the return for all the effort. Don't let this happen to you.

Choose Metrics that Matter

To make sense of a pricing change, you need to look beyond a single metric or moment in time. That's why we use the FBC Model, a simple but powerful framework that helps you assess impact through three distinct lenses:

- **Financial outcomes.** Is the business in a stronger commercial position?
- **Behavioural responses.** How are customers reacting in practice?
- **Confidence within the team.** Can we apply and explain pricing clearly and confidently?

Each lens tells a different part of the story. Together, they bring clarity to what's working, what's not and where to go next, and they help you close the loop between strategy and performance.

Let's explore each lens in turn.

Financial Outcomes

Financial outcomes are usually the first place leadership looks when assessing whether pricing has worked. These indicators tell you whether the business is earning more per customer, protecting its margins and unlocking greater long-term value.

Headline revenue growth, however, can be misleading. A jump in sales might come from a one-off volume spike or unrelated activity. That's why it's important to look beyond a single figure and consider how a broader set of financial indicators are moving over time. Are margins recovering after a long decline? Have steadily growing volumes suddenly slowed? By paying attention to trends, rather than just totals, you can see whether your pricing decisions are truly shaping a stronger commercial position.

Taken together, these metrics offer a clear view of whether your pricing strategy is delivering sustainable commercial gains:

- **Revenue per customer.** Are you earning more per transaction or contract?
- **Gross margin.** Have changes led to healthier profitability?
- **Average order value.** Are customers opting for higher-value options?
- **Sales volumes.** How sensitive has demand been to price changes?
- **Discounting trends.** Are you holding the line on value or eroding margin?

Strong financial performance doesn't just validate your pricing decision. It also funds the next phase of growth.

Behavioural Responses

Once you've assessed commercial performance, the next question is: how are customers reacting to the new pricing? Numbers might be up, but without behavioural context, you can't tell if pricing is building long-term value or creating future risk, such as a drop in customer loyalty.

This lens helps you spot how pricing is influencing customer decisions, from how they evaluate options to whether they remain loyal customers. You're looking for patterns in behaviour that signal acceptance, resistance or hesitation. It's where you start to notice if customers are walking away, trading down or leaning into higher-value offers.

You're looking for patterns in behaviour that signal acceptance, resistance or hesitation.

- **Conversion rates.** Has uptake improved, stayed flat or dropped off?
- **Churn and retention.** Are the right customers sticking around?
- **Customer lifetime value.** Are customers spending more or less over time?
- **Product mix.** Are customers buying different types of products or services?
- **Sales cycle length.** Has pricing helped speed up or slow down decisions?

Changes in customer behaviour are often early indicators of pricing success or signals that adjustments may be needed. Before diving into internal sentiment, this view gives you essential clues about how your market is responding.

Confidence Within the Team

Confidence is the bridge between your pricing strategy and what actually happens in front of customers. If your teams aren't sure how to talk about pricing, they'll hesitate, default to discounts or avoid the conversation altogether.

The confidence lens helps you assess whether your commercial, product and support teams are equipped to use pricing in the way it was intended. It's about how well teams follow the playbook, how confidently they justify the price and whether they raise issues proactively or quietly work around them.

- **Sales team adoption.** Are teams using the new pricing with confidence?

- **Discounting discipline.** Are guardrails being followed or bypassed?

- **Customer support queries.** Has pricing become a source of confusion or clarity?

- **Team sentiment.** Are internal conversations about pricing grounded in evidence?

- **Decision-making speed.** Has pricing helped or hindered momentum?

Confidence like this is hard to fake but easy to observe. When pricing is working, handoffs are smoother, debates are shorter and the team moves faster. When confidence is low, everything slows down.

The signals you collect through the FBC model allow you to consistently measure, interpret progress and decide what to do next. Instead of drowning in data, focus on the indicators that truly reflect your pricing goals and can be tracked reliably over time.

To help you apply this thinking in practice, we've summarized the three lenses (Figure 11.1). Use this table to guide your team in choosing the right indicators to watch and avoid getting lost in the noise.

Let's go back to Pour & Prosper Coffee Co.

After raising prices on their core drinks menu and introducing new bundled offers, the CFO was eager to understand what impact it was having. They needed a simple way to make sense of what was happening and used the FBC Model to pick just two indicators from each lens to guide their thinking.

Lens	What It Tells You	What to Look For
Financial Outcomes	Is the business in a stronger commercial position?	Revenue per customer, margin, average order value, customer Lifetime Value (LTV)
Behavioural Responses	How are customers responding to the new pricing?	Conversion, churn, upgrades/downgrades, decision speed, objections
Confidence Within the Team	Can your team implement and explain confidently and consistently?	Adoption by sales, discipline on discounts, support tickets, sentiment, velocity

Figure 11.1 The FBC Model.

From the **Financial** lens, they chose *average transaction value* and *gross margin*. These showed whether the business was earning more from each sale and the impact on the bottom line.

From the **Behavioural** lens, they looked at *customer retention* and *order mix*. They wanted to know if regulars were still coming in and whether customers were trading down, sticking with their usual or exploring higher-value options.

From the **Confidence** lens, they tracked *barista confidence* and *complaints at the till*. Each week, they held informal check-ins with staff to see how they felt talking about the new prices and whether pushback from customers was increasing or easing off.

That was it. Six indicators to enable the team to see what was working, spot early concerns and make smart, timely adjustments.

They didn't need complex systems or dashboards. By focusing on the metrics that mattered, the team could stay close to what was happening and make confident, well-informed decisions.

With the right indicators in place, the next step is knowing *when* to track them. To get a true picture of what your pricing is achieving, you need a clear rhythm for when to check in as well as what to look for. That's where we go next.

Decide When to Measure

Not all results show up overnight. Some effects of a pricing change will surface quickly. Others will unfold more gradually as customers renew, upgrade or change behaviour over time. Setting the right measurement rhythm ensures that you catch early signals without rushing to judgment, and track long-term trends without losing momentum.

We recommend checking in at four key milestones: immediately after launch, after 30 days, 90 days, and again at 180 days. Each of these milestone checkpoints is designed to surface specific types of insights relevant to your current stage.

We also suggest layering in a regular cadence of reviews between these milestones and building them into your team calendar from day one. These should be structured working sessions to review the metrics you've selected to track. For example:

- Daily huddles in the first week to catch any teething issues
- Weekly check-ins during the first month to spot emerging trends
- Fortnightly reviews between days 30 and 90 to keep up momentum, track stabilizing patterns and adjust early assumptions

- Monthly reviews after 90 days to monitor long-term shifts in customer behaviour and financial performance
- Interim checkpoints as-needed after 180 days

Of course, if something unexpected emerges between formal checkpoints (like a spike in churn or sales anomalies), hold an ad hoc meeting to investigate and act. Figure 11.2 outlines this roadmap.

Figure 11.2 The 180-Day Pricing Impact Roadmap.

Launch Week

Mindset.
Think of this as a soft landing check. You're not expecting major performance shifts yet, but you are looking for bumps in the road that could derail momentum.

What to review.
- Are there any technical issues or surprises in how pricing is being applied?
- Are customers reacting as expected?
- Are your support or sales teams fielding unexpected questions?

What to watch out for.
Jumping to conclusions. A few reactions don't equal a trend, but ignoring them can let a small issue spiral out of control.

One-Month Review

Mindset.
Enough time has passed to begin spotting early trends, but you're still in the learning phase.

What to review.
- Are conversion rates holding, climbing or dipping?
- Are customers gravitating to certain options?
- Are there any signs of customer resistance or churn?

What to watch out for.
Over-indexing on edge cases. Use the data to identify patterns, not outliers.

Three-Month Review

Mindset.
At this point, you can step back and assess the impact with more confidence. Trends have begun to stabilize, and early behaviours have had time to play out.

What to review.
- How is performance tracking across different customer types or channels?
- Are price-related objections increasing or decreasing?
- Has customer sentiment changed?

What to watch out for.
False attribution. Make sure you separate pricing impact from other concurrent initiatives like product changes or promotional activity.

Interim Checkpoints After Six Months

Mindset.
You're no longer in evaluation mode, you're in evolution mode. The pricing change is now part of business as usual. It's time to reflect, refine and decide what's next.

What to review.
- Have key financial metrics moved in the right direction?
- Has the team maintained discipline and confidence?
- What would you keep, change or expand based on what you've seen?

What to watch out for.

Drifting from discipline. Pricing often softens over time as teams revert to old behaviours. Reinforce the rationale and tools that support your current approach.

At Pour & Prosper Coffee Co., the team followed a simple, structured rhythm to continue learning from their pricing change and make adjustments along the way.

Immediately after launch, they ran a soft landing check. On day two, the staff noticed customers hesitating at the counter, uncertain about the new bundles like Kickstart Combo, Fuel Up and Coffee4Two. Decision times grew longer, and a few regulars asked pointed questions. Instead of panicking, the team updated their in-store signage and provided baristas with a brief cheat sheet to explain the options with confidence. By the end of the week, conversations were smoother and sales had stabilized.

At the 30-day mark, they reviewed early sales trends. One pattern stood out: the Kickstart Combo, a coffee and pastry bundle, was significantly outselling the others. Meanwhile, the higher-priced Fuel Up bundle, which included a breakfast sandwich, coffee and banana, was being overlooked. The owner realized the value of this option wasn't coming through clearly. They added a small countertop sign highlighting it as 'Fuel Up: Protein-packed, barista-backed. Perfect post-workout' and coached staff to suggest it to customers who looked like they'd just come from the gym. Uptake of Fuel Up began to climb.

After 90 days, the picture became clearer. The team noticed that occasional customers were returning less frequently, but loyalty card data showed that regulars were still visiting just as often, some even more frequently. When they dug deeper, it became clear that the price change had a more substantial impact on price-sensitive visitors but hadn't dented loyalty from their core audience. They made a plan to introduce seasonal offers to re-engage more price-conscious customers, while continuing to strengthen value for their most loyal fans.

At 180 days, the pricing shift had become part of how their coffee shops operated. The team reviewed their key financial metrics and saw a sustained increase in both average transaction value and gross margin. Staff confidence had remained steady, and the team was enjoying explaining the bundled offers. Most importantly, customer LTV had grown, and regulars were spending more over time. With solid results and stronger team buy-in, the leadership team began exploring how to apply the same tiered approach to catering and wholesale orders.

Pricing isn't a set-and-forget decision. Even the simplest change deserves a clear, thoughtful rhythm of review. The coffee shop didn't rely on complex systems or wait for perfect data. They watched closely, listened carefully and made small, smart adjustments at each stage. That's how they turned a pricing experiment into a foundation for long-term growth.

Having a regular cadence of check-ins helps you stay close to what's happening and make timely adjustments. Still, no single metric or moment tells the full story. Pricing impact can build gradually and is often combined with other commercial efforts. That's why it's worth stepping back to ask the bigger question: is the business in a better position than before? A clear rhythm of review gives you the insight to answer that with confidence, without needing to isolate every last variable.

Attribute the Impact

Attributing the impact of a pricing change is more than a technical challenge. It is a behavioural and political one. Pricing doesn't come with a flashy campaign or a glossy interface, so when growth appears, it's easy for others to claim the win. Without clear evidence, pricing becomes invisible.

That's why you need to get ahead of the narrative.

Attribution helps you protect the integrity of your pricing work.

You've already identified the signals that matter most and mapped out when to review them. Now it's time to plan how you'll attribute the impact to pricing vs. other factors. This will give you the tools to tell a clear, confident story when the numbers come in. Attribution helps you protect the integrity of your pricing work and strengthens your ability to learn and adapt.

Here are five practical ways to do it:

1. **Revisit your hypotheses**

   Before the launch, you made some assumptions about how customers would respond, such as who would accept the change, where pushback might occur and what success would look like. Now's the time to test those expectations against what actually happened. Checking back against your original thinking helps you understand which results were genuinely driven by pricing and which may have come from elsewhere. It's a simple way to ground attribution in intent rather than guesswork.

2. **Track other moving parts**

   To understand what pricing really influenced, you need to know what else was happening at the same time. Product updates, seasonal shifts, marketing campaigns, sales pushes and competitor moves can all affect performance. Keeping a simple, shared record of these activities gives you essential context when attributing results and helps you separate pricing impact from everything else.

3. Look across different groups

Compare how pricing landed with different customer groups, such as new vs. existing clients. You can also compare outcomes by region, channel or sales team where other variables have remained relatively stable. If you ran pricing experiments, bring those results into the mix. These contrasts help you spot where pricing made the biggest difference and avoid overcrediting or underestimating its role.

4. Visualize the mix effect

When performance improves or declines, it is rarely due to a single factor. Use a simple waterfall chart to show how various contributors like pricing, volume changes, product mix, currency fluctuations or cost changes have shaped the overall result. A graphical visualization helps you illustrate attribute impact more clearly and shows stakeholders how pricing fits into the broader picture. Figure 11.3 shows how a £500K revenue increase was broken down into volume gains, pricing uplift, product mix and other influencing factors. Even a rough estimate builds trust and supports more balanced conversations.

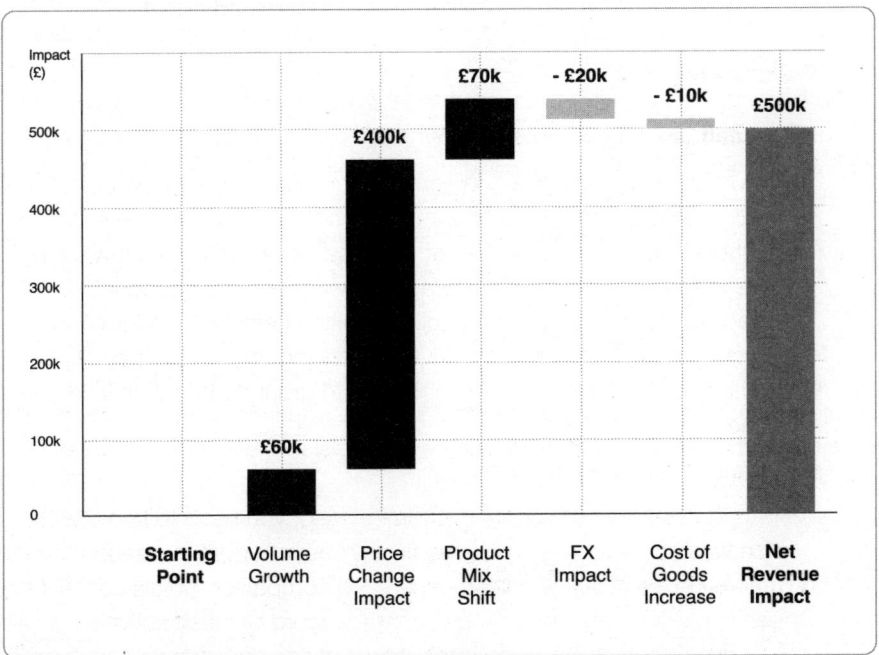

Figure 11.3 Illustrative pricing attribution waterfall.

5. Pair signals with stories

Data gives you the signals, but stories reveal the context. Quotes from salespeople, customer comments and support queries can reveal how pricing is showing up in real conversations. These real-world reactions help you explain the why behind the numbers, making your attribution story more human and more persuasive.

At Pour & Prosper Coffee Co., attribution became just as important as the pricing change itself. As results matured, the leadership team knew questions would follow. Sales were up, but this could be because a new office building just opened down the block from one of their most profitable cafes. Gross margin had improved, but they'd also renegotiated supplier contracts mid-quarter. Without a clear view, it would have been easy to lose confidence in what pricing had actually delivered.

To stay ahead of the story, the team revisited the signals they had chosen up front and mapped these against other business activity. They logged the supplier change and the local foot traffic spike, then looked across customer types to isolate where pricing had made the clearest difference.

They saw that improvements were strongest in areas directly linked to pricing. Bundled drinks were driving higher margins, and customers were responding positively to the refreshed offers. Baristas felt more comfortable explaining the pricing, and queries at the till had dropped. Importantly, uptake of the Fuel Up combo had grown steadily after the signage and staff coaching, and well before the new office opened up.

To bring the data to life, the team paired these signals with stories from the shop floor. Baristas shared moments where regulars reacted well to the new options, or asked fewer questions at the till. These anecdotes helped illustrate what the metrics alone could not: a pricing shift that felt natural, not forced.

By connecting the dots clearly and credibly, the team was able to isolate the role pricing had played. It wasn't the only factor, but it was a decisive one. With both the numbers and the stories to back it up, they could claim the win confidently at their next board meeting and use it as a springboard for what came next.

That's why attribution matters. It's not just about defending your pricing work. It's about shaping the narrative, guiding what your team and stakeholders take away from the experience, and making sure decisions are judged on evidence, not assumption.

Plan Your Next Step

Attribution builds confidence. It makes future pricing work easier to propose, easier to support and more likely to succeed. So the next time someone asks what really made the difference, you won't need to speculate. You'll have both the data and the story to show them.

As you look back at the impact of your price change, ask yourself:

- What role did pricing actually play?
- What evidence are you using to support that view?
- How will you make pricing performance more visible next time?

Attribution is about making sure your biggest growth lever is recognized, understood and ready to keep delivering.

Don't let pricing become the unsung hero of your business.

Don't let pricing become the unsung hero of your business. Make it visible. Make it accountable. Most of all, make it count.

Next, we'll look at how to turn this momentum into something more permanent, building pricing into the rhythm of your business, not just as a project, but as a capability.

PRICING PLAYBOOK: MEASURE THE IMPACT

Here are seven steps to help you measure the impact of pricing.

1. **Build measurement into the mix**
   Build measurement into your pricing process from the start, not as an afterthought. It's how you capture the win and show that pricing works.

2. **Select what to measure**
   Use the FBC Model to assess the impact through three lenses: Financial outcomes, Behavioural responses and Confidence within the team. Together, these tell a clear story of performance.

3. **Choose metrics that matter**
   Pick a small number of indicators that align with your pricing goals. Focus on what's relevant, trackable and easy to explain.

4. **Set a rhythm for review**
   Measure at key intervals: immediately and 30, 90 and 180 days post-launch. Use each stage to spot signals, test assumptions and stay on course.

5. **Track signals and stories**
   Combine data with real-world feedback. Pair your metrics with customer and team anecdotes to build a richer picture of what's really happening.

6. **Isolate the role of pricing**

   Separate pricing from the noise. Track what else changed during your rollout and compare across customer groups to strip out other variables. Focus on where pricing made a clear, measurable difference.

7. **Claim the win**

   Don't let pricing become invisible. Use attribution to shape the narrative, build internal confidence and make future pricing work easier to support.

12
BUILD THE PRICING MUSCLE

At the start of this book, we talked about the weight of uncertainty that so many leaders carry when faced with pricing decisions. Think back to where you were then: the questions, the hesitation, the guesswork. How different does pricing feel now?

You have prototyped, validated, nudged, tested and made decisions grounded in evidence rather than instinct. You've taken pricing from something reactive to something deliberate. Most businesses never get this far. If you've completed your first Pricing Sprint, you've done what most teams put off, delay or avoid entirely.

Your next challenge is different: keeping the momentum going. Many teams quickly slide back to old habits. They revert to reactive pricing decisions, make a single change and stop there, or wait until the next crisis forces their hand.

We have seen this play out many times. One CEO told us, 'After the sprint, we felt energized and aligned. But 6 months later, pricing had slipped down the list, and we were scrambling to react to a market that had already moved on. We knew we should have kept it front of mind.'

Pricing isn't something you do once and forget. Customer needs evolve. Competitors reposition. Costs shift. Even the value you deliver can change over time. To keep pace, your pricing must be just as dynamic.

Pricing isn't something you do once and forget.

Left unattended, pricing quickly loses its edge and with it, margin, momentum and market opportunity. But with steady practice and the right rhythms in place, it becomes one of the most resilient and impactful tools in your business. Pricing is often the lever that teams forget to maintain (or worse, only ever pull as a promotional mechanism), but you've already proven you're not like most teams.

This final chapter is about helping you shift from pricing as a one-off project to establishing it as a lasting business capability. We'll show you how to build on the work you've done and embed pricing as a strategic lever and core competency in your business, supported by clear roles, repeatable habits and a cadence that ensures pricing maintains a seat at the strategy table.

Shift from Project to Practice

As Pour & Prosper Coffee Co. reached the end of their Pricing Sprint, the team had clarity on questions that once felt murky. They now understood why their prices had changed and what value they were delivering. Their baristas could speak with confidence about what made their seasonal roasts special. Their online store featured a clear, intuitive pricing structure, supported by behavioural nudges that guided customers toward higher-value options. They had tested price points, anchored their offerings and gathered feedback from customers who felt heard, not blindsided.

Now the team faced a choice: take a breather and hope the hard work sticks . . . or build the habits that would make pricing a lasting growth lever.

Let's explore both paths.

Down the first path, the team feels proud and rightly so. The new pricing is live, feedback is positive and early results look good. They turn their focus to other priorities: a new wholesale partnership, an upcoming product launch. Then 3 months later, the cost of green coffee beans have spiked, and a new competitor has opened two streets over, undercutting them with a $4.25 latte.

Suddenly, they're in firefighting mode. 'We did all this work,' the head of ops says, 'but before long, things shifted, we weren't ready, and we had to rebuild the thinking from scratch.'

This is what happens when pricing is treated as a one-off project. You get a moment of clarity, but no rhythm to maintain it.

Now, taking the second path, Pour & Prosper builds a lightweight pricing rhythm. Every month, they set aside 30 minutes to review pricing performance alongside product, sales and cost data. They revisit customer feedback and run small, low-risk pricing experiments on new seasonal bundles and monthly subscriptions. One person is clearly accountable for pricing, not to do all the work alone, but to champion it in every conversation.

When conditions shift, the signals are already on the radar. Bean prices rise? They've seen the trend. Competitor undercutting? They've already tested a loyalty offer that customers love.

This is what pricing capability looks like. When changes are needed, conversations start early and adjustments are timely, measured and strategic. The team has confidence that pricing is working as hard as it can, week by week, quarter by quarter.

In the organizations that treat pricing as a core discipline, we've seen three foundational Rs at play:

- **Roles.** Clear ownership of pricing decisions and activities, so it's never a question of 'Who's responsible for this?'
- **Rhythms.** Regular, structured moments where pricing is reviewed, challenged and improved. These create rhythm and accountability.
- **Resources.** A set of tools that allow for regular review and reporting, keeping decisions focused on evidence, not gut feel.

These three Rs form the backbone of pricing capability. In the rest of this chapter, we'll break each one down and show you how to embed them in your own business.

Define Roles

In many organizations, no one truly owns pricing. It often sits across teams like commercial, operations, finance, strategy or marketing. With no truly accountable owner, everyone assumes someone else is looking after it, until a problem surfaces and the scramble begins.

To build pricing into a lasting business capability, you need to start by defining roles.

Defining roles does not always mean creating a dedicated team or hiring a specialist. Some businesses may not have the resources or need to build a standalone pricing team. For others – particularly when pricing complexity is high, different markets require different approaches, or pricing already plays a central role in growth and profitability – establishing a dedicated team can be both impactful and practical.

But what if you're not there yet?

This section is for businesses that lack formal pricing capabilities but are ready to treat pricing as the strategic lever it truly is. This may mean that there is no formal pricing role in place. Or, the individual responsible for pricing may operate in an advisory or analytical capacity only, without the commercial remit or political influence needed to drive change. In these situations, assembling a Pricing Board is a smart first step. Think of it as your launchpad: a way to establish clear ownership, build internal alignment and secure early wins that position pricing as a strategic priority.

At the centre of the Pricing Board is a Pricing Champion who is responsible for keeping pricing visible, intentional and regularly discussed. Supporting them is a cross-functional group that brings diverse perspectives from across the business. While pricing decisions may be shaped collaboratively, ultimate sign-off rests with a senior leader who holds overall commercial accountability. Let's look at a baseline for who is Responsible, Accountable, Supporting, Consulted and Informed (RASCI).

Responsible: Pricing Champion

The person who keeps pricing moving. They coordinate quarterly reviews, manage updates to pricing strategy and ensure that experiments, feedback and insights are shared across teams. They don't own every task, but they do own the operating rhythms that make the pieces of the pricing puzzle fit together. They need to be senior enough, or have enough internal credibility, to bring teams together, drive collaboration and turn conversations into action.

Accountable: Senior Decision Maker

Pricing is ultimately a commercial decision. The senior decision maker is the one who holds final accountability to sign off major changes to pricing and ensures it supports the broader financial and strategic goals of the business.

Supporting: Pricing Board

This is a cross-functional group made up of roles from product, sales, marketing, operations and finance. This team supports the Pricing Champion by contributing data, customer insights and frontline experience to inform decisions. When forming your Pricing Board, use the same principles outlined in Chapter 1: keep it small, cross-functional and empowered. Involve senior voices who can move quickly, challenge assumptions and mobilize others to act.

Consulted: Subject Matter Experts

These are the people whose expertise the Pricing Board relies on to make sound decisions. This group is brought in on an as-needed basis to test assumptions, validate ideas or support implementation. For example, someone from the legal team ensures that proposed changes are compliant and low-risk. Representatives of the customer success and sales teams may offer a ground-level view of how customers are responding or where friction is building.

Informed: Delivery Teams

This group needs to stay in the loop so pricing changes can be implemented smoothly. They're the ones who bring pricing to life, whether that's updating systems, automating pricing rules, building a price calculator or translating pricing into messaging, visuals and frontline conversations. They don't shape pricing decisions, but they do bring them to life, ensuring everything is aligned, accurate and on-message.

Create Operating Rhythms

Where the roles define *who* is involved in pricing, operating rhythms define *how* they work together.

Operating rhythms turn individual ownership into collective capability. They create regular moments, built into the normal pace of the business, where pricing is deliberately discussed, tested and improved.

These operating rhythms don't need to be long or complicated. This could be a 30-minute monthly check-in or a 90-minute quarterly pricing review alongside your sales and product retrospectives. What matters most is that they happen so that pricing has a regular rhythm and doesn't fall between the cracks.

These rhythms help you:

- **Spot early signals** when something's changed in costs, customer behaviour or the competitive landscape.

- **Ask the right questions**: Is our current pricing still aligned with the value we deliver? Should we rethink pricing before our next launch? Can we run an experiment to test a new hypothesis?

- **Reduce decision pressure** by spreading pricing work into smaller, regular steps rather than high-stakes, once-a-year debates.

- **Shape culture** so pricing has a seat at the table and is seen as a critical lever for commercial growth.

Operating rhythms can take different forms depending on your business model, team structure and pace of change. Let's look at a few examples to help you start designing a rhythm that fits your business.

Regular Price Reporting

Price reporting lays the foundation for informed and timely decisions. It's about establishing a regular cadence to surface key data points and spot early signals. These may include margin trends, customer feedback, pricing performance by segment or whatever metrics best relate to your pricing strategy. Periodically, it's also worth looking for hidden opportunities in the data you don't regularly review (see Chapter 2 for ideas).

Price reporting is often prepared and analysed outside of meetings. However, sharing it in advance of meetings with the Pricing Board, along with key observations and discussion points, ensures that everyone arrives informed, reduces meeting time and builds shared context across teams.

Monthly Pricing Check-In

A short, structured, monthly check-in keeps pricing visible and top of mind. The agenda can rotate each month based on need, depending on the pricing experiments you are running or changes you are seeing in the market. The goal is consistency to keep pricing present, even when it's not urgent. Check-ins are largely tactical and ideal for maintaining momentum, spotting early signals and deciding what needs deeper attention.

Quarterly Pricing Review

Quarterly pricing reviews are cross-functional discussions designed to zoom out and assess what's working, what's shifted and where to focus next. These are best run alongside quarterly sales or product retrospectives and may include performance metrics, a review of the overarching pricing experimentation roadmap, and any upcoming pricing dependencies such as upcoming releases of new products or features.

Pricing Retrospective

While monthly check-ins and quarterly reviews help you stay on top of emerging trends, a retrospective gives your team space to step back and make sense of what a pricing change really delivered. It brings together financial outcomes, customer behaviours and internal confidence to shape your next move. Done consistently, it helps your team sharpen instincts, adjust assumptions and improve decisions with every cycle. See Chapter 11 for guidance on when and how to measure the impact of price changes.

Annual Pricing Appraisal

Annual pricing appraisals serve as a deep dive into your overarching pricing strategy. What's changed in your offering that might affect how it's valued? What's changed in the market? Where might margin or willingness to pay be slipping? What pricing moves should you consider to stay aligned with your growth goals? This is about keeping your pricing in step with the wider strategy, so every commercial lever is working towards the same outcome.

Bringing in someone external for this process can offer a valuable outside perspective. Fresh eyes can challenge assumptions, surface blind spots and highlight opportunities that might be easy to overlook from inside the business. Whether it is a specialist consultant, a trusted advisor or even a peer in your network, an external voice can help bring sharper focus and renewed clarity to your pricing strategy.

Prepare Resources

Roles define *who* is involved, operating rhythms define *how* they work together, and resources provide the *tools* to keep everything moving.

Even the sharpest team with the best operating rhythms can't make confident pricing decisions if they don't have the information they need. The right data at the right time can help surface signals, spot shifts and answer the big commercial question: is our pricing still working?

Every business will need a different set of tools depending on its model, sales volume and complexity. Ownership of those tools will vary based on your team's capabilities and how you've structured your Pricing Board. But the goal is the same: to bring clarity, consistency and speed to pricing conversations.

Let's look at some practical tools your team can build to make sure pricing decisions remain based on evidence.

Competitive Price Index

This tool benchmarks your pricing against key competitors, whether that's comparing prices of specific SKUs, categories or overall price positioning. It's most powerful for businesses with visible competitor pricing (e.g. e-commerce or direct-to-consumer), where automated price scraping tools or manual audits can be used to keep an up-to-date picture.

For some service-based businesses and those with unpublished pricing, the approach is more qualitative. You'll most likely capture intelligence from customer feedback, sales conversations or secret shopping.

If you're just getting started, keep it simple: track three to five of your most relevant competitors (identified through research) and focus on key price points or product areas. Update your index regularly, with a frequency that reflects how often prices change in your industry. This might mean daily, weekly, quarterly or annually, depending on your market dynamics and pace of change.

See Chapter 2 for more on competitor price tracking.

Price Configurator

The price configurator is a practical calculator that applies pricing logic to help you set consistent, strategically aligned prices. It offers a snapshot of your current pricing structure, while also allowing you to simulate different pricing logic and test different rounding strategies (such as .95 or .45) to ensure that price presentation feels right.

You can use it to price new products using your existing hierarchy and model the likely impact of any price changes under consideration. It can estimate factors like financial impact, break-even volume and how your prices compare in the market.

Price Change Log

A price change log is a centralized record of all pricing changes. Include what changed, when, why, for whom, how it was communicated, and the impact on the business and customers. It's especially helpful in fast-moving teams, where memory fades quickly or decision makers change. Tracking the rationale behind pricing changes builds accountability and serves as a valuable long-term reference point for future work.

Experimentation Tracker

A lightweight tool for tracking your roadmap of pricing experiments, past and future. For past experiments, track what you tested, with whom, where, and what happened. For future experiments, track the intended tests in the same way along with any dependencies that need to be met before the test can be executed.

Your experimentation roadmap serves as a log of pricing experiments. It helps you build institutional memory, compare results over time and avoid rerunning the same test twice. Start simple, even in a spreadsheet. Over time, you can build this into your broader testing cadence or integrate it with product or marketing roadmaps.

Deal Conversion Tracker

This tool is most useful for companies with high-touch sales processes, especially in B2B environments where deals are complex and decisions are consultative. It helps teams capture what's really driving purchase decisions by logging data from won and lost deals including reasons for buying (or not), objections raised, competitor activity and deal structure details.

In B2B, insights often come from sales conversations or proposal reviews. In B2C, where the sales cycle is shorter, they may surface through exit surveys, live chat transcripts or feedback forms. Over time, this creates a clear picture of what's resonating, what's getting in the way and how pricing is influencing outcomes.

Price Change Evaluator

The Price Change Evaluator is a tool for analysing the impact of a pricing change by looking at before-and-after results in your business data. Instead of needing a strict control group (like you would in an A/B experiment), it uses historical comparisons to judge whether the change worked.

This brings rigour to pricing trials, support decisions to scale, revert or adjust, and feed learnings into future experiments.

Protect the Strategy

Pricing capability isn't just about setting smart prices. It's about protecting them when it matters most. That's what separates teams who use pricing as a strategic lever from those who slide back into reactivity.

Once you have the people, rhythms and resources in place, the real test of your pricing capability comes when the pressure is on, when sales are behind target, or when a competitor makes a move that rattles the team.

The real test of your pricing capability comes when the pressure is on.

Someone asks, 'Can we just make an exception?' Someone else says, 'Let's just discount it this time and figure the rest out later.'

In those moments, all the clarity you built can start to wobble. Just one change, one time, to make the deal work. Yet, this is precisely how discipline begins to slip.

So as you continue, keep coming back to the tools you already have in place:

- **You have a clear North Star Goal.**

  Use it to anchor trade-offs to long-term impact, not short-term panic.

  Ask: Does this move get us closer to that goal, or just help us survive the week?

- **You have a clear pricing strategy.**

  Use it to weigh options against your broader positioning and value proposition.

  Ask: Is this decision consistent with the pricing strategy we've agreed on?

- **You've set pricing guardrails.**

  Use them to stay within agreed boundaries and avoid unplanned exceptions.

  Ask: Are we making a deliberate decision or breaking our own rules?

- **You've built a shared language.**

  Use it to make decisions together and back each other when it's time to hold the line.

  Ask: Are we all telling the same story and ready to stand behind it?

- **You've embedded data into decision-making.**

  Use it to guide the conversation, challenge assumptions and reduce knee-jerk reactions.

  Ask: What does the data tell us?

- **You know how to learn from customers.**

  Use insights from price testing, surveys and interviews to avoid guessing under pressure.

  Ask: How might we validate this with customers?

- **You know how to run a Pricing Sprint.**

  Use the roles, rhythms and resources you've established to surface new opportunities, turn them into hypotheses and focus your next sprint on what matters most.

  Ask: Is this a sign we need a new Pricing Sprint to solve a new problem?

The strongest pricing teams aren't the ones who get it right once. They're the ones who stay calm, stay curious and adapt with intention under pressure. Trust the decisions you've made. Your strategy wasn't a guess, it was backed by evidence. Protect it with confidence, because price integrity is much harder to rebuild than it is to maintain.

Trust the decisions you've made.

Why it's important to protect the strategy

Without discipline, even a well-evidenced strategy can be undone by short-term pressure. That's precisely what happened to a fast-growing retail business that did everything right, until the pressure set in.

The team spent months reworking its pricing, and at launch the results of their hard work were immediate: higher margins, improved conversion and more transparent value communication. Internally, the team felt confident. Externally, the market responded.

Just a few months later, new business slowed. Dashboards of data were being produced, but no one originally involved in the pricing decisions was responsible for interpreting them, let alone acting on them. The company began to come under pressure from the board. With no one championing the strategy they worked so hard to build, it was quickly overridden by the CEO, who introduced an across-the-board discount 'just until things pick up'.

It wasn't a failure of pricing. It was a failure of discipline. The team hadn't built the rhythms or clear accountability that would allow them to recognize the early signals and respond with intention to the trends they were seeing. Without the muscle to back their decisions, the business reverted to old habits.

The outcome? Margins shrank, and the pricing team found themselves picking up the pieces of the strategy all over again.

Adapt as You Grow

Holding the line doesn't mean refusing to change. It means knowing when to stand firm and when to evolve. The pricing that helps you win your first 100 customers is rarely the same pricing that will sustain profitable growth, attract investment or support a successful exit. Pricing should evolve in line with your goals, your maturity and the market around you.

There will come a point in every business when it's time to ask: is pricing doing the job we need it to today, or are we still using yesterday's logic?

In the early stages of building a business, pricing is often about learning. The aim is to reduce friction, build momentum and get meaningful feedback. At this point, accessibility may matter more than margin. As one founder put it, 'We priced to get people through the door. Every sale was a critical case study.'

As the business grows, priorities shift. You may have reached product-market fit and now need pricing that funds expansion. Perhaps you are building deeper relationships with your core customers and want to reflect more value through premium offers or account growth. Pricing becomes a tool for influencing what people buy, how long they stay and how much value they generate over time. The focus moves from acquisition to retention, margin and customer lifetime value.

Then there are moments of reinvention. A business facing rising costs, new competition, or falling demand may need to move quickly to recalibrate. In these cases, pricing becomes a survival tool. We have seen businesses simplify their offers, refocus on the most profitable segments or introduce upfront payment models to improve cash flow. These decisions are not just tactical. They are based on being clear about what the business needs most at a specific point in time.

At the other end of the journey, a business preparing for sale may use pricing to demonstrate to buyers that margins are defensible, revenue is predictable and

When you're clear on what pricing needs to accomplish, it becomes one of the most powerful levers available.

customers see the value in what they are paying for. In due diligence, these signals give acquirers confidence that the business can sustain its performance and justify a stronger valuation.

Wherever you are – launching, evolving, stabilizing or preparing to exit – when you're clear on what pricing needs to accomplish, it becomes one of the most powerful levers available.

PRICING PLAYBOOK: BUILD THE PRICING MUSCLE

Here are six steps to help you build the pricing muscle in your organization:

1. **Shift from project to practice**
    Treat pricing as an ongoing discipline. Keep the momentum going by building habits that extend beyond your first Pricing Sprint.

2. **Define clear roles for pricing**
    Make it clear who leads, who contributes and how pricing decisions get made across the business.

3. **Create operating rhythms**
    Use regular rhythms to keep learning and improving.

4. **Prepare the tools to monitor and measure**
    Put in place practical tools that help you track progress, spot opportunities and make better pricing decisions.

5. **Protect your strategy**
    Use the strategy you've built to stay confident under pressure and avoid reactive decisions.

6. **Know when to adapt**
    Revisit your pricing as your goals shift. Make sure it's doing the job your business needs.

BE THE PRICING CHAMPION

If there's one thing we hope you take from this book, it's that pricing is one of the most powerful tools you have to shape your business, reflect your value and drive sustainable growth. It's also the lever most teams overlook. Most wait too long, change too little or default to what feels safe, even when it holds them back.

We need more pricing champions. People who ask the uncomfortable questions. People who are brave enough to test, to listen, to learn.

We need more pricing champions.

People who treat pricing not as a one-off project but as a commercial discipline that evolves with the business, and helps steer it forward.

That can be you.

You've already done the hard part. You've made pricing visible. You've gathered the evidence, shaped the conversations and taken confident action. Now, keep going. Make it part of your operating rhythm. Keep it at the heart of how you make decisions and create value.

You've uncovered a strategic superpower that's been hiding in plain sight. This is your chance to embed pricing into the fabric of how your business thinks, decides and grows. Stand by the value you've built, and help your team do the same.

When you champion pricing, you don't just influence revenue and profitability. You forge deeper connections with your customers and instil a shared sense of value, purpose and commercial courage across your business.

Now that's priceless.

WHAT'S NEXT

This book has equipped you with the tools, strategies and confidence to turn pricing into your secret weapon for growth. We hope you're feeling energized and ready to put your Pricing Sprint into motion.

Of course, every sprint looks different, and it's normal to hit roadblocks along the way. If you find yourself needing expert input or a partner to lead your sprint from start to finish, we'd love to help. Visit **untappedpricing.co.uk** or get in touch at **sprint@untappedpricing.co.uk** to explore how we can work together.

If you're looking for ready-to-use tools, templates and practical resources to support your sprint, head to **thepricingsprint.com**.

ACKNOWLEDGEMENTS

We've found that the best outcomes emerge when people are willing to listen openly to one another, test ideas early and work through trade-offs together. That's what the Pricing Sprint is really about: collaboration in action. It's not the tools that make the difference; it's what they enable. They create space for teams to listen more closely to their customers *and* one another. They help shift the goal from simply selling more stuff to designing solutions that people truly value. And they invite teams to explore new ideas with openness, curiosity and creativity.

This book reflects that same process. It's the result of many minds, many iterations and many moments of learning that played a role in shaping what you have read.

You'll find examples and stories throughout these pages drawn from our experience working with clients, interviewing their customers, collaborating with our team, sparring with other experts and speaking day in and day out to business leaders of all shapes and sizes. We've changed names, adjusted details and in some cases blended examples or introduced fictional scenarios. These edits allowed us to focus on clarity, flow and lesson sharing, without compromising confidentiality. Where we've been explicit about the client we worked with, we had permission to do so. In every case, the goal was the same: to make the tools and lessons easy to understand and apply to your own business.

Thank you, Untapped team

This book is the culmination of years of collaborative work, field experiments and a shared commitment to developing pricing strategies that benefit both businesses and the people they serve. To the entire team at Untapped Pricing, a heartfelt thank you. Your talents, keen insights and daily work helped shape and stress-test this methodology long before we knew it would ever hit the shelves.

Luke Battye, Maaike Mintjes and Josie O'Donovan, thank you for your sharp thinking, lived experience and generous reviews of this manuscript.

Special thanks to Rick Mather and Kate Thompson; your expertise and strategic thinking are infused into the DNA of the Pricing Sprint. You are true masters of your craft.

Thank you, clients
Thank you for trusting us with your team, your business and your customers. You were the earliest champions and the bold testers of the Pricing Sprint approach. You brought the real business challenges that make this methodology sound in theory and workable in practice. This book wouldn't exist without your trust, your ambition and your willingness to partner with us to make bold business decisions. We're grateful to be part of your journey.

Thank you, manuscript reviewers
Emma Kamel, Tom Tweddell, Emma Tweddell and Tom Ball, your encouragement gave us a boost when we needed it, and your insights helped us see where clarity, structure or tone could land even better.

Thank you, creative and publishing partners
A special thank you to our book coach Ameesha Green for your guidance and sharp editorial instincts throughout the writing process. Your calm clarity helped us stay focused, find our voice and trust the story we were here to tell.

Lisa Wright, thank you for designing a book cover that embodies the energy, momentum and collaboration of a Pricing Sprint. You transformed folded paper into a striking work of art, creating a powerful visual metaphor and a beautiful invitation to open the book and explore what lies within.

To Giacomo Bottoli, thank you for creating the images and diagrams throughout this book. Your eye for detail and skill in creating engaging visuals added another layer of impact to this work.

To the team at Bloomsbury Business, thank you for championing this project from pitch to publication. Your editorial care and guidance helped shape this book into something we're truly proud of.

Thank you, family and friends
Thank you, Brian Padley, James Millar, Gillian Crisp and all our family and friends for your patience, ideas and unwavering support. For every early morning, late night, paused holiday or late dinner delayed by the words 'just one more paragraph', thank you. You gave us the space, support and encouragement to bring it to life. We couldn't have done this without you. Thank you, Ben and Jack Millar, for your creative minds, constant encouragement and Lego tributes that made us smile. Your support from the sidelines means the world.

QUICK REFERENCE GUIDE

Use this quick reference guide to revisit the steps of The Pricing Sprint anytime you need a fresh perspective on your pricing.

EXPLORE

DESIGN

REFERENCES

Chapter 2

[1] Calandro, Joseph, and Scott Lane. 2007. 'A new competitive analysis tool: the relative profitability and growth matrix.' *Strategy & Leadership* 35 (2): 30–8. https://doi.org/10.1108/10878570710734516

Chapter 3

[1] Schwab, Katharine. 2017. 'Ideo Studied Innovation In 100+ Companies—Here's What It Found.' Fast Company. https://www.fastcompany.com/3069069/ideo-studied-innovation-in-100-companies-heres-what-it-found
[2] Knapp, Jake, John Zeratsky and Braden Kowitz. 2016. *Sprint: How to Solve Big Problems and Test New Ideas in Just Five Days*. Bantam Press.
[3] Ariely, Dan. 2008. *Predictably Irrational: The Hidden Forces that Shape Our Decisions*. Harper.

Chapter 4

[1] Coulter, Keith, and Robin Coulter. 2005. 'Size Does Matter: The Effects of Magnitude Representation Congruency on Price Perceptions and Purchase Likelihood.' *Journal of Consumer Psychology* 15 (1): 64–76. https://doi.org/10.1207/s15327663jcp1501_9
[2] Coulter, Keith, Pilsik Choi and Kent Monroe. 2012. 'Comma N' cents in pricing: The effects of auditory representation encoding on price magnitude perceptions.' *Journal of Consumer Psychology* 22 (3): 395–407. https://doi.org/10.1016/j.jcps.2011.11.005
[3] Thomas, Manoj, and Vicki Morwitz. 2005. 'Penny Wise and Pound Foolish: The Left-Digit Effect in Price Cognition.' *Journal of Consumer Research* 32 (1): 54–64. https://doi.org/10.1086/429600
[4] Wadhwa, Monica, and Kuangjie Zhang. 2015. 'This Number Just Feels Right: The Impact of Roundedness of Price Numbers on Product Evaluations.' *Journal of Consumer Research* 41 (5): 1172–85. https://doi.org/10.1086/678484

[5]   Cialdini, Robert B. 2021. *Influence, New and Expanded: The Psychology of Persuasion*. HarperCollins.

[6]   Ariely, Dan, George Loewenstein and Drazen Prelec. 2003. '"Coherent Arbitrariness": Stable Demand Curves Without Stable Preferences.' *The Quarterly Journal of Economics* 118 (1): 73–106. https://doi.org/10.1162/00335530360535153

[7]   Bertrand, Marianne, Dean Karlan Sendhil Mullainathan, Eldar Shafir, and Jonathan Zinman. 2010. 'What's Advertising Content Worth? Evidence from a Consumer Credit Marketing Field Experiment.' *The Quarterly Journal of Economics* 125 (1): 263–306. https://doi.org/10.1162/qjec.2010.125.1.263

[8]   Iyengar, Sheena S., and Mark Lepper. 2000. 'When choice is demotivating: can one desire too much of a good thing?' *Journal of Personality and Social Psychology* 79 (6): 995–1006. 10.1037//0022-3514.79.6.995

[9]   Iyengar, Sheena S., Gur Huberman and Gur Jiang. 2004. 'How Much Choice is Too Much? Contributions to 401(k) Retirement Plans.' In *Pension Design and Structure: New Lessons from Behavioral Finance*, 83–96. Oxford University Press. 10.1093/0199273391.003.0005

[10] Chernev, Alexander, Ulf Böckenholt and Joseph Goodman. 2012. 'Choice overload: A conceptual review and meta-analysis.' *Journal of Consumer Psychology* 25 (2): 333–58. https://doi.org/10.1016/j.jcps.2014.08.002.

[11] Tversky, Amos, and Daniel Kahneman. 1974. 'Judgment under Uncertainty: Heuristics and Biases.' *Science* 185 (4157): 1124–31. 10.1126/science.185.4157.1124

[12] Heidhues, Paul, and Botond Kőszegi. 2004. 'The Impact of Consumer Loss Aversion on Pricing.' *WZB Discussion Paper*, No. SP II 2004-17.

[13] Tversky, Amos, and Daniel Kahneman. 1981. 'The Framing of Decisions and the Psychology of Choice.' *Science* 211 (4481): 453–8.

[14] Thaler, Richard H. 1999. 'Mental accounting matters.' *Journal of Behavioral Decision Making* 12 (3): 183–206. https://doi.org/10.1002/(SICI)1099-0771

[15] González, Eva M., Eduardo Esteva, Anne L. Roggeveen and Dhruv Grewal. 2016. 'Amount off versus percentage off—when does it matter?' *Journal of Business Research* 69 (3): 1022–7. https://doi.org/10.1016/j.jbusres.2015.08.014

[16] Kolenda, Nick. 2025. 'The Psychology of Pricing: A List of Tactics for Marketers and Retailers.' *Kolenda Marketing Psychology*. https://www.kolenda.io/guides/pricing

[17] Puccinelli, Nancy M., Rajesh Chandrashekaran, Dhruv Grewal and Rajneesh Suri. 2013. 'Are Men Seduced by Red? The Effect of Red Versus Black Prices on Price Perceptions.' *Journal of Retailing* 89 (2): 115–25. https://doi.org/10.1016/j.jretai.2013.01.002

Chapter 5

[1]   Vargo, Stephen L., and Robert F. Lusch. 2004. 'Evolving to a New Dominant Logic for Marketing.' *Journal of Marketing* 68 (1): 1–17. https://doi.org/10.1509/jmkg.68.1.1.24036

[2]   Almquist, Eric, John Senior and Nicholas Bloch. 2016. 'The Elements of Value.' *Harvard Business Review* (September). https://hbr.org/2016/09/the-elements-of-value

[3] Almquist, Eric, Jamie Cleghorn and Lori Sherer. 2018. 'The B2B Elements of Value.' *Harvard Business Review* (March–April).

[4] Fitzpatrick, Rob. 2013. *The Mom Test: How to Talk to Customers and Learn If Your Business is a Good Idea when Everyone is Lying to You*. CreateSpace Independent Publishing.

Chapter 6

[1] Ramanujam, Madhavan, and Georg Tacke. 2016. *Monetizing Innovation: How Smart Companies Design the Product Around the Price*. Wiley.

[2] Green Carmichael, Sarah. 2014. 'The Silent Killer of New Products: Lazy Pricing.' *Harvard Business Review* (September). https://hbr.org/2014/09/the-silent-killer-of-new-products-lazy-pricing

[3] Lipovetsky, Stan. 2006. 'Van Westendrop Price Sensitivity in Statistical Modeling.' International Journal of Operations and Quantitative Management 12 (2): 141–56.

[4] Gabor, André, and C. W. J Granger. 1966. 'Price as an Indicator of Quality: Report on an Enquiry.' Economica 33 (129): 43–70. https://doi.org/10.2307/2552272

[5] Louviere, Jordan J., Terry N. Flynn and A. A. J. Marley. 2015. *Best-Worst Scaling: Theory, Methods and Applications*. Cambridge University Press.

[6] Reid, Leopold, Stephanie Eckerd and Lutz Kaufmann. 2022. 'Social desirability bias in PSM surveys and behavioral experiments: Considerations for design development and data collection.' *Journal of Purchasing and Supply Management* 28 (1). https://doi.org/10.1016/j.pursup.2021.100743

[7] Stewart, Jennifer M., Eamon O'Shea, Cam Donaldson and Phil Shackley. 2002. 'Do ordering effects matter in willingness-to-pay studies of health care?' *Journal of Health Economics* 21 (4): 585–99. https://doi.org/10.1016/S0167-6296(02)00003-6

[8] Krosnick, Jon A. 1991. 'Response strategies for coping with the cognitive demands of attitude measures in surveys.' *Applied Cognitive Psychology* 5 (3): 213–36. https://doi.org/10.1002/acp.2350050305

Chapter 8

[1] Stickdorn, Marc, Markus Hormess, Adam Lawrence and Jakob Schneider. 2018. *This is Service Design Doing: Applying Service Design Thinking in the Real World: A Practitioner's Handbook*. O'Reilly Media.

Chapter 9

[1] Ferguson, Jodie L., and Pam Scholder Ellen. 2013. 'Transparency in Pricing and Its Effect on Perceived Price Fairness.' *Journal of Product & Brand Management* 22 (5/6): 404–12. https://doi.org/10.1108/JPBM-06-2013-0323

[2] Checkout process for the Turbo Levo 4 Pro at *specialized.com* (accessed March 2025).

Chapter 10

[1] Kahneman, Daniel, and Amos Tversky. 1979. 'Prospect Theory: An Analysis of Decision under Risk.' *The Econometric Society* 47 (2): 263–92. https://doi.org/10.2307/1914185

[2] Ruggeri, Kai, Sonia Alí, Mari Louise Berge et al. 2020. 'Replicating patterns of prospect theory for decision under risk.' *Nature Human Behaviour* 4 (May): 622–33. https://doi.org/10.1038/s41562-020-0886-x

[3] Ferguson, Jodie L., and Pam Scholder Ellen. 2013. 'Transparency in Pricing and Its Effect on Perceived Price Fairness.' *Journal of Product & Brand Management* 22 (5/6): 404–12. https://doi.org/10.1108/JPBM-06-2013-0323

ILLUSTRATIONS

INDEX

Provenance 170–1
psychological nudges 16
The Psychology of Pricing (Kolenda) 65
purchase behaviour 15, 108

quality control 97–8
qualitative research 99,113
quantitative research 73, 116, 131
quarterly pricing reviews 128, 204
quiet steals 28–9

RASCI (Responsible, Accountable,
    Supporting, Consulted, Informed)
    201–2
Reddit 162
red herrings 28–9
research recruitment agencies 75
risk tolerance 48
Ritz-Carlton 149
role definition 201–2
'Rolls-Royce customers' 125

sales teams 29, 189
sales training 128
sampling 97, 179–80
secret shopping 205
Segmentation Surveys 92
segmenting strategy 76, 120, 135
senior decision-makers 8–9
service-based businesses 62, 143
Service-Dominant Logic 72
social desirability bias 111
social proof 60, 67, 218
software 2, 25, 32, 46, 82, 120, 125, 156
Sprint Valley (strategy consultancy) 66
subscription services 82, 120, 139–40,
    160, 165
subscription vs. pay-per-use 86–7

target prices 26–7
teams 7–10, 12–20, 110–13, 189
testing
    A/B 117–19
    cohort 118, 120–2

conclusions 122–3
full-scale 118, 121–2
multivariate 117, 119, 122
option suppression 126
price-presentation experiments
    124–5
price-promotion experiments 123–4
retention promotion 124
testable hypotheses 18
value-add promotion 124
'test and learn' programme 66
This is Service Design Doing (Stickdorn)
    134
time-tracking apps 72–3
trade-offs 15, 74, 93, 107, 110, 207
*Transparency in Pricing and its Effect on
    Perceived Price Fairness*
    (Ferguson/Ellen) 156
triangulation 134–6
Trustpilot 60, 162

'unapologetic change' narrative 177–8

validation
    at scale 114
    introduction 91
    price-setting 141
value
    customer perception of 109, 210
    'difference' narrative 178
    drivers 108, 110
    messaging 40, 47
    perception of 71–3, 100
    understanding what drives 107
    value-driven approach 137, 141–2
Van Westendorp, Peter H. 103
Van Westendorp Price Sensitivity Meter
    81–2, 100, 102–5, 111, 114

Walmart 149
WellSpend Health (example) 116–17,
    121–2, 136, 138, 143,
    147
WhatsApp 175